# God Has Gone Corporate

Jenness Reid

*www.worksoftrinity.com*

Published by Works Of Trinity, LLC
Teaneck, New Jersey, 07666, U.S.A.
www.worksoftrinity.com

All scripture quotations are taken from The Holy Bible, King James Version (KJV) – *public domain*.

No part of this book may be reproduced or transmitted in any form or by any means; electronic or mechanical – including photocopying, recording, and information storage and retrieval systems; without written permission from the publisher. Send email to: permission@worksoftrinity.com.

*God Has Gone Corporate*

Copyright © 2014 Jenness Reid, all rights reserved.

Commissioned by Jesus Christ

ISBN-13: 978-0-9831999-4-6 (paperback)
ISBN-13: 978-0-9831999-5-3 (electronic)
Library of Congress Control Number: 2014916535

# Dedication

This book is dedicated to Jesus Christ of Nazareth (Yeshua HaMashiach). He directed me to go into business for God (Adonai) by requesting that I write books for Him.

# Disclaimer

Everything in this book relates to my experiences with The Trinity (God, Jesus, and the Holy Spirit) as They prepare me to establish Their business. The names of actual individuals and places have been changed for identity reasons.

This book is for educational purposes only, and only you are responsible if you choose to do anything, based on what you read.

Jenness Reid

# Contents

| | |
|---|---|
| Preface | 6 |
| A Rare Star Is Born | 13 |
| Connections with Jesus' Bride | 23 |
| Is Corporate God a New Concept? | 36 |
| Finding A Business Name | 41 |
| The Colors of God's Business | 44 |
| The Display of God's Color | 56 |
| God's Logo for Works Of Trinity | 69 |
| The Story of This Book Cover | 81 |
| The Marketing Environment | 91 |
| God's Special Marketing Strategy | 97 |
| Divine Connections | 107 |
| My Job Preview | 117 |
| The House of God | 130 |
| A Special Editor | 141 |
| Holy Spirit Fire | 147 |
| An Existing Star Is Called | 157 |
| Giving Tribute to God in Songs | 165 |
| The Joshua Connections | 170 |
| Joshua's Anointing | 184 |
| Aftermath of the Anointing | 198 |
| The Mighty Hands of God | 211 |
| Spiritual Disruption: Unleashing the Next Wave of Saving Souls | 216 |
| Bibliography | 249 |

# Acknowledgement

I would like to acknowledge the help of God (Adonai), Jesus Christ (Yeshua HaMashiach), and the Holy Spirit (Ruach HaKodesh) in providing guidance as I act on their behalves in putting the business of Works Of Trinity together. They have made Divine contributions to this book by providing its content, through my experiences with Their works.

I give special acknowledgement to my editor, Patsy Quashie. May the favor of God be on her life.

# Preface

The reader will come to realize that God has commissioned me to establish a commercial business for Him so that He will get the attention of all people in the world. Everywhere people are caught up in economic gains, or struggling to survive the economic crisis. In such atmosphere, God is often taken out of the picture.

This book tells the stories of how God directed me to go into business for Him, with the Trinity [God (Adonai), Jesus Christ (Yeshua HaMashiach), and the Holy Spirit (Ruach HaKodesh)] as Directors. It sets the tone for God's corporate image so that secular corporations will come to understand "*Who*" has entered the marketplace.

In writing this book, I consulted with the Holy Bible to compare how God was using people to do His business in those days. There are references to God's business in both the Old and New Testament. In the Old Testament, the Levites were appointed as officers for specific territories to execute the business of the Lord God (1 Chronicles 26:30). Some were given the task of executing business external for God's house while others oversaw the internal aspects of God's business (Nehemiah 11:16; 11:22).

In the New Testament, at the age of twelve, Jesus knew He must take care of God's (His Father's) business. Later the apostles had the task of dealing with how to conduct God's business. In that, positions existed for seven men who were honest, wise, and full of the Holy Spirit to take on the business of ministering to the Grecian widows (Luke 2:49). Paul encouraged the Romans to be industrious in doing God's business and fervent in spirit when serving God (Romans 12:11).

In the Bible, references to God's business point to managing the affairs of the church, which includes sharing God's words, bringing souls to God, and taking care of the poor and needy. The new, radical approach God has to enhance the works of the church is to enter the corporate world in such a way that secular businesses have to pay attention to Him. The corporate world is one area on which Satan has taken a stronghold. The dream I had on November 13, 2011 is an indication of this.

I dreamt, *I was engaged in spiritual battle with an evil spirit when it started speaking. It said it was the head of all evil spirits.*

*I then found myself at a place looking at a spread of land. The evil spirit continued to speak and said it controlled the music industry, drug business, education,...* I was awakened as I felt it was trying to assault me, sexually.

The above dream indicates the areas where The Holy Spirit of God will have me do work for Him. Satan can identify those who God elects to do special works for Him and will therefore try anything to stop them. From my experiences, I learned that Satan will attack you in the areas where God intends to use you. This evil attack in the dream indicates that God intends to use me to represent Him in the corporate world and Satan was trying to prevent this from happening.

Since Satan has entered the corporate world and has been creating havoc with the economy – worldwide, God Himself will address this problem. He will reverse the work of Satan as He brings people to Him and deliver them from their afflictions.

An example of how God will reverse the work of Satan was given to me in a dream. On January 3, 2001, I dreamt, *I was sitting in a meeting with some people; most of whom I didn't know. However, one was a co-worker. I noticed a very young black man to the right of me. I knew* he was doing internship at the company and he was the nephew of my co-worker.

A man was at the podium. My co-worker spoke to him and said, "Remember what I told you about my nephew. You need to keep him employed. I can show you why." A lady from the audience walked up to the podium with a lap top. I realized she too was related to the young man. She opened the lap top and started to show pictures of the young man. Most of the pictures were of him with his family in different settings.

The lady then showed a video with the young man on the street. He was passing by a group of other young black men who were acting in a way that was typical of young black men – walking with a unique style, while listening to music. One of the young men in the group was bobbing his head a lot as he listened to the usual street type music. I could tell this group of young black men on the street used to be friends of my co-worker's nephew. However, my co-worker's nephew just looked at them and passed by. I could tell he had decided he would no longer be a part of that crowd.

The Holy Spirit of God gave me this dream to demonstrate the kind of changes He is going to make in society, as He goes corporate in a very visible way. The music industry is an area of grave concern to God since it has such great influence on people – especially young people.

God has allowed me to set up His corporate business to effect the changes He will be making in the world's economy and in society. People have been very distracted with the many economic crisis and the stress it brought on them; not to mention the changing attitudes of the workplace where there is the tendency to overwork employees due to the advantage of job shortage and the desire to increase profit. This situation has affected people's relationship with God. They have become more focused on accumulating wealth or surviving the economic crisis and less focused on God – their Creator.

I have had personal experiences where The Holy Spirit showed His displeasure with me when I was rushing through my prayer to quickly get back to doing work that I had brought home from the job. I was reading prayers from Charles Capps book, *God's Creative Power: Will Work For You*. To show His displeasure with me, The Holy Spirit stopped me on the word, *"harmless"* in the following sentence, *"I bind and cast down spiritual wickedness in high places and render them harmless…"* (Capps 28).

*Preface*

I could not speak or get up from my knees for about one hour. After The Holy Spirit released me, I turned off the work computer in shame and apologized to God for giving Him less time in order to try to survive in this economic era. From my personal experience, I know that what has been happening with the economic conditions and changes in the workplace have not escaped God's attention. God will be speaking the language of *"commerce,"* which is understandable across all languages. People will come to know of the existence of the Almighty God who created humankind, after He starts to make His works in that area obvious.

In preparing me to go into business for Him, The Holy Spirit of God took me though different stages. I have been through the dream stage in which The Holy Spirit gave me many dreams that were fulfilled. These are written about in my book, *God Works Through Dreams*. The next stage is God's mission. In this, there was outright spiritual warfare in which I was fighting various forms of spiritual battles which prepared and qualified me to do His business. These experiences are written about in my book, *God's Mission: Spiritual Battles and Revelation of Anti-666*. I have now entered the business stage in which God is going corporate to handle the economic crisis and the crisis of the soul. Many people have gone astray, and more people are heading in the direction of Hell than Heaven (Zambrano).

    This book focuses on the aspect of my spiritual journey in which The Holy Spirit of God guided me in establishing His business. The Trinity – God (Adonai), Jesus Christ (Yeshua HaMashiach), and the Holy Spirit (Ruach HaKodesh) – are the Directors of this business – Works Of Trinity, LLC.

*Chapter 1*

# A Rare Star Is Born

On November 24, 2010 a new star was birthed in the galaxy of the corporate world as Works Of Trinity, LLC became incorporated. The decision to incorporate was not an easy one. I had not done any business courses in college and have a history of starting business ventures and then giving them up due to lack of knowledge, time, and cost constraints.

In 2010, I had a visitation from Jesus Christ, in the Spirit, which started in a dream and continued into my awakening. In this visitation, I heard myself promising Him to write His books. We had a long conversation, through my spirit, in which I was agreeing with Him and making promises to Him by responding with the word, "*Yes.*" Jesus controlled the conversation as Spirit to spirit so that my mind would only know that I promised to write books for Him and that I have made many other promises to Him (Reid---"God's Mission").

When I was faced with the challenge of incorporating a business for Jesus Christ, it must have been one of the unknown promises (to the mind) that I made to Him. Jesus has unique ways of reminding me of my promises to Him. After I drafted the first two manuscripts for Jesus' books, I started doing research into publishers that offered self-publishing.

I had the idea of being an author with a website that promotes my books. This way, I would not have to think of having employees. However, in the process of signing up with a self-publishing company, God led me to a printing company. The idea of having a company with greater control of the printing process and higher profit margin from the sale of my books was formed. In this way, I could truly develop a Divine, spiritually-based company, which contributes to the economy by hiring relatives and others to conduct God's business. I knew God put this challenge of going into business for Him, in my spirit.

Putting the pieces of the puzzles to form Works Of Trinity had not been easy for me because during all this I had to maintain a full-time, demanding job. During my two weeks' vacation in 2010, I decided to double my efforts to move the process along. Being my own publisher began to weigh heavily on me. I decided to ask my daughter, Kristal, if she would be my Customer Service Manager. She told me that she had other plans. I got discouraged.

On November 23, 2010, I was contemplating giving up the idea of being my own publisher, which is much more complicated than the alternative of being just a self-published author. With the self-published author alternative, I would use a publishing company, which would pay me royalties. I wouldn't have to spend much time running the business.

I recognized I needed to go into fasting to get quick answers from God, since time was short, and I had seen where He was directing me to be my own publisher. I decided to pray about which direction to take His business. In the morning, I did half a day fasting and prayed to God for guidance in making this crucial business decision. At noon, I again repeated the prayer and then went outside to clean leaves from the yard.

While outside, I saw a car drove up and parked on the road, alongside my property. A young white man came out with a book in his hand. I stopped the leaf blower as he started to walk down my driveway. He came up to me and told me he worked on my house more than four years ago. I then recalled who he was. The young man said he had borrowed a book and was returning it. I asked him if he was finished reading it. He said, *"No, but I will get if from the library."* I took the book from him and read the title. It read, *"Things Fall Apart."* I handed it back to the young man and told him to keep it, since I would not be using it. I asked him how business was doing, and he said, *"Not too good."*

After the young man left, I realized that this was a spiritual incident. It was more than four years ago since he borrowed the book from my house. Just after finishing my prayers for God to give me direction as to whether I should change my mind about becoming my own publisher, He sent this young man as a messenger to let me know His plans for me would fall apart if I go the way of being just an author. If I am to be my own publisher, as God intended, the stories that He is and will be authorizing me to write would not be subjected to alterations by a publisher to fit what they consider to be more socially acceptable stories about Him and His works.

God has a way of setting up things, way ahead of time. Whatever tempted that young man to borrow the book more than four years ago turned out to be part of God's plan to use him as a messenger to me, right *"on time."* God urged the young man to return the book, as an answer to my prayer. After this spiritual incident, I felt confident in taking the more difficult path of becoming my own publisher – the way God had directed me, previously.

As I put the pieces of the puzzle together to form Works Of Trinity, LLC, I continued to fast and pray for God's input. On November 24, 2010, I went to the farmer's market to buy string beans that my sister, Ruth, asked me to buy. She said the ones she saw in her neighborhood were not looking good.

When I returned from the farmer's market, I saw the local newspaper in the driveway. I picked it up and was about to throw it in the paper recycling container when I thought it was bulkier than usual; maybe I should quickly see if there were any interesting sales in it. This was very unusual for me since I was always busy and would not pay much attention to the paper. However, I was on vacation and had a little more time.

On the first page of the newspaper, I saw the headline, *"Arts center proposed for vacant site."* It was not an interesting title, but I decided to read it anyway. It was news about the former site of a fragrance company in my town which was up for sale and the town was seeking to convert it into an arts center. The president of the town's Chamber of Commerce envisioned the building being used as a community-based performing arts center and the town's chamber could be headquartered there where it could help small business, especially those that were home-based. This would give them a street address for mail delivery, copying and office facilities and conference rooms that they could rent (Prosnitz).

I knew it was a spiritual incident which led me to decide to read the town's paper and to find the article about home-based business that directly speaks to my need. This was God's way of encouraging me. If Ruth had not asked me to buy string beans I would not have come out of the house, since I was busy setting up God's business. However, by leaving the house, I saw the town's newspaper and read the news of a facility that could accommodate the business. This was *on time* information and yet another immediate answer to my prayers related to the setting up of God's business. I knew God was directing me in the way I should take His business. He certainly answered my prayer very quickly. He knew I only had two weeks in which to setup His business before I return to work. I went ahead and submitted information to a company that provides business incorporating service. They accomplished the work of birthing the rare star – Works Of Trinity, LLC.

The incorporation of Works Of Trinity, LLC is an indication that God has chosen to go into the business of gathering the lost and healing the wounded in ways that everyone will see His works and acknowledge them. God, Himself will be going after His children and they will come to know Him (Ezekiel 34:8-31). Therefore, Jesus Christ has commissioned me to establish God's company as a radically different way of reaching out to the lost – using the language of commerce that all understand and give attention. Works Of Trinity, LLC is supposed to continue one or more of the works of Jesus Christ by doing good, teaching in the churches, proclaiming the gospel of the kingdom, healing all manner of sickness and diseases from people, and casting out devils from people who are possessed (Acts 10:38; Matthew 4:23-24).

Although Jesus Christ died to save us, not all of us have accepted Him. Some have chosen to continue to be deceived by Satan. Despite this, Jesus devised another plan to give people the chance to accept the salvation He brought to us. As the Trinity (God, Jesus, and The Holy Spirit) enters the commercial marketplace in an obvious way, people will have to pay attention to what affect their daily survival. It will no longer be, *"follow what is happening on Wall Street."* It will be, *"follow what is happening with The Trinity."* As Works Of Trinity, LLC moves forward in business with its logo symbolic of Jesus Christ – the bright *"red"* rare star whose blood was shed to save us – the world of business will never be the same again.

Through dreams and spiritual incidents, God showed me some of the function His *"rare star"* would be performing when executing His work on earth. Through movements of the Holy Spirit, God is allowing me to keep my promise to Him to help others who are experiencing *"spiritual wickedness"* – like what I had experienced. Like the logistical movement of a star, God has been allowing me to use movements of my hands to locate sources of spiritual wickedness and shoot the arrow of God's reversal of wickedness to bring deliverance to myself and others. The final design of God's business logo speaks to its intent. It came about after February 18, 2012, when I overheard a conversation about the death of Whitney Houston which led me to the story of John Todd.

From John Todd's article, I learned that the Star of David was known before as the Hexagram or the Crest of Solomon; that when witches are practicing witchcraft they would get in a five-pointed star within a circle (their strongest form of protection) and place a six-pointed star within a circle beside it. This arrangement is supposed to cause demons to appear at their instructions (Todd).

I must admit that it was frightening to read this since I immediately realized what God was preparing me to go up against – those that practice witchcraft and similar crafts. However, I was determined not to fail God; I finalized His logo according to His desire so that Satan will know that Works Of Trinity, LLC is a company under God's control. God will be responsive to His logo in bringing about deliverance to those who are spiritually afflicted.

Although I have been given the task of establishing God's business, I know that one day Jesus Christ will come in person to take control of it. I had two dreams that led me to this conclusion.

On November 8, 2010 I dreamt, *God gave me a business bag and told me, "It must be modern." I immediately passed it on to Jesus. In a later dream, I saw Jesus came down from the sky through the clouds along with a half-hidden body. I next saw Him walking and holding a little girl's hand. I realized that the little girl was me.* Jesus, being represented by the big red star in God's business logo, will come to not only lead me, but to take full control of God's established company – the *"rare star"* in the corporate world.

Works Of Trinity is indeed a *"rare star"* that has been birthed. However, I do not believe it will be the only *"rare star,"* but I only know of my story. Many rare stars will be produced; as in alignment with what is happening in the galaxy. A rare star-making galaxy, called Baby Boom, is generating an unusual number of stars all at once ("Rare star-making galaxy found").

*Chapter 2*

# Connections with Jesus' Bride

God placed it in my spirit that He asked me to go into business for Him because of His disappointment with the churches. Since then, I have heard many confirmations that God is dissatisfied with today's churches – from visiting pastors at my church; sermon by a pastor in The Bahamas in 2011; and Barbara Yoder at Matt Sorger's conference (Yoder).

God is getting ready to revamp the way the churches are operating so they will be more focused on Him, not conformed to the world, and really seek after sinners the way He wants them to. God does not have pleasure in the death of sinners. His desire is for them to turn from their sinful ways and live (Ezekiel 33:11; 15-16).

With Divine connections, God confirmed my thinking that He will establish such a public image with His business of saving sinners that He cannot be ignored. He would be doing this through the corporate business He allowed me to establish for Him. God knows that I am not a Biblical scholar. I have not been diligent with reading the Bible. Yet, He chose to use me. Throughout my new walk with God, Jesus Christ has been developing me spiritually, from scratch. I can relate my spiritual growth to a dream I had *of dining with a Jewish family and the sister telling me that the wife made the milk from scratch, after I commented on how good the milk tasted* (Reid---"God Works Through Dreams").

Jesus controlled my spiritual growth so that at the stage of launching God's business, whatever I speak on His behalf must come directly from Him. I cannot inject myself into any of His work; otherwise I would not know how to pull it off. I had never stood up in church and read the Bible during church service until 2010, neither did I attend Bible classes. Furthermore, verbal communication in a group setting has always been a weakness my past and current supervisors have commented about. Knowing this, I told God I would do whatever He wants me to do as long as He is doing it Himself, through me – according to the operating agreement of Works Of Trinity, LLC. In this, The Holy Spirit inserted a statement that the company will *"carry out activities as authorized by the Trinity – God,*

*Jesus, and the Holy Spirit.*" The insertion incident happened when I did a draft of what I wanted to add to the operating agreement template at one insertion point. With one paste action and at one point of the cursor, God allowed the words to be copied to two different places instead of the one place I had intended.

God addressed my concern, as I thought I was not traditionally trained to carry out His ministry (business). By using Divine spiritual incidents, He showed me that He would be carrying out the works Himself, through me. In other words, no man-designed training is needed since God will be doing all the works, through me. The Divine spiritual incidents that led me to this conclusion started with a phone call from my daughter, Kristal, in August of 2011 while she was on vacation. As I was talking to her I could hear the sound of waves in the background. I thought she was on the beach. She too heard the sound and asked, "*What is that noise?*" I responded by asking her if she was not on the beach and she said, "*No.*" The thought came in my spirit, "*God wants me to go on vacation.*"

I did not give further thought to the idea of going on vacation. I had my vacation planned but intended to stay at home and finish my writing. However, the next day after the Divine incident with the unexplained noise of the beach over the phone, God confirmed the idea that I should really go away on vacation. My co-worker, Mark, came to me and asked me if I could switch my vacation week with him since they do not allow too many employees in the same group to go on vacation at the same time. When he asked me this, I knew God was using him to confirm that I should go away on vacation. I had a timeshare which was expiring at the end of the year, but I did not plan to use it.

Because of Mark's request, I decided I would just go ahead and use the timeshare. I told Mark I would go ahead and do vacation research using the dates he wanted to switch and then let him know if I could do it. This promise forced me to stay up late that night and checked out timeshare exchanges and flights for the desired dates. The only English-speaking island available for the desired timeshare exchange dates was in The Bahamas. I did the exchange and booked my flight.

On November 11, 2011, roughly three weeks before my vacation date, I dreamt, *I was at the beach but not in the water. I saw a bride and a groom, dressed in white, came out of the sea and passed by me on my left. Next the bridal party, dressed in blue, came out of the sea and passed by me on my left.*

*I then looked toward the water. There were people swimming. Suddenly the water became rough and started making huge waves – about twelve feet tall. People started to come out of the water. A young girl from my church did not seem to be concerned about what was going on although she was in the water, in a small water-floating device. I went and pulled her out and told her she had to get out.*

I knew I should pay attention to this dream and God would bring its meaning to light, while I was on vacation. I had no idea how this dream would be fulfilled but my first guess was something to do with wedding.

The fulfillment of the dream unfolded in an unexpected way. I had ordered DVDs from Matt Sorger's Ministry, for a conference I had attended. I saw someone looking like me on the cover of the advertisement, which triggered my desire to buy the set. The DVD set came the day before I was to go on vacation, so I decided to take them with me.

The first night I was at the timeshare resort in The Bahamas, I had to call for help to figure out which button to use to switch from TV to DVD mode. It was not obvious. When the maintenance worker saw it was a sermon DVD, we started talking about religion. I told him I wanted to go to church the next day and he invited me to his. My dream of bride and groom coming out of the sea was fulfilled at this church.

During the sermon, the pastor spoke of *"The Next Great Move Of God,"* which is, *"A Church Without Walls."* She spoke of the earth being filled with the knowledge of God as the waters cover the sea (Isaiah 11:9), of a son being born who would be the head of government (Isaiah 9:6-7), of a church that will establish the government of God on earth, and of God constructing a church without walls to display His glory on earth. She referenced the story of God showing Ezekiel water coming out of a house where His altar was located. From the different locations on the property, water was measured. At first, water reached Ezekiel at his ankle, then at his knees, then at his loins, and then it became a river he could not pass over (Ezekiel 47:1-5). At this point in the sermon, I recalled the dream I had of the waves at the beach going from normal to very high.

Much later in the service, the pastor referred to the church as being God's bride. I knew then for sure that my pre-vacation dream was being fulfilled in a verbal way at this church, as I heard this sermon with mentions of varying levels of water and of a bride. In addition, the wife of the resort worker was young and resembled the young girl in the dream. I knew God wanted me to link this sermon to what I was writing in His book, since I have been having some Divine incidents related to bride.

Based on the sermon involving water and my dream connection to it, I decided to read Ezekiel chapter 47 to see what I should use from it. However, I found the story started in earlier chapters. I kept on going back to previous chapters to find the beginning of the story. My reading led me to chapter 33 and there I found what God really wanted me to use.

In Ezekiel chapter 34, God confirmed my thoughts that it will really have to be Him directly working through me to execute the works He predestined for me. I knew God was concerned that the church was not performing as He expected. I also knew the work He had planned for saving souls was a radically different approach from traditional churches. God's concerns for the functioning of the church and the vision of His new church can be illustrated in the revelation He gave to Ezekiel regarding His dissatisfaction with the rulers of Israel in the way they were taking care of His children.

God asked Ezekiel to prophesy to the leaders of Israel that as shepherds they did not care about their sheep (children of God), only about themselves; they did not strengthen the diseased, heal the sick, bandage the broken ones, bring back those that went astray, and they did not seek after the lost; but instead ruled them with cruelty. The behaviors of God's shepherds caused His sheep to be scattered and to be destroyed by wild animals. The sheep wandered about while the shepherds did not seek to find them. The sheep became prey while the shepherds took care of themselves.

God turned against the shepherds and decided that He would take away His sheep from them and would never let them become shepherds over His sheep again. These shepherds would only be allowed to take care of themselves. God Himself would seek after His lost sheep and those driven away. He would find them, deliver them from all the places they had been scattered, bring them to their own land, and feed them in Israel in good pasture. God promised to bandage the broken sheep, strengthen the sick ones, and destroy the rich and strong and pass judgment on them. God would then judge His sheep, separate the good from the bad, make a covenant with them, cause evil to cease from among them, and allow them to live in safety. God would then bless His sheep, the earth would yield plenty of food, and the sheep would feel safe and know that God is their Lord Who delivered them.

God promised to raise up a plant so that there would no longer be any hunger among His sheep. They would know God is with them. The sheep are God's children (Ezekiel 34:2-31).

Church leaders who are not shepherding God's children properly should take heed. I was told of a rabbi in New York who recognized Jesus Christ as the true Messiah but did not share this with his congregation. Instead, he reads both the Old Testament and New Testament of the Bible – thinking he cannot break tradition, but will save himself. This rabbi needs to take heed of the vision of a pope in Hell because he did not instruct his followers that they should go to God through Jesus Christ and not through Jesus' mother – Mary (Zambrano). Because of dissatisfaction with church leaders, God is calling for a new breed of people who will not let religion get in the way of doing His work.

On September 19, 2015, in doing my final book edit, I saw that I had written, *"Jesus Christ gave John a vision about the church as His bride."* God had me paused here and recheck the Revelation 21. I prayed to God for help in what I was writing because I realized He wanted me to change it. I fell asleep with the Bible resting on my shoulders, opened to Revelation 21, and the computer on my legs. I woke up and saw the time – 3:33 a.m.; waking up at 3:33 a.m. caused me to realize what change I need to make to my earlier writing. Jesus' bride is not the existing churches on earth, but a new one that will come directly from Heaven, at the time of His return. God himself will be dwelling in it with His people. It will be the *end-of-time* church when there is a new Heaven, a new earth, and no more death (Revelation 21:1-3, 9-27).

I knew long ago that I had to incorporate writing about Jesus' bride in this book because of the many experiences I had of Divine spiritual incidents involving marriage. I know that the company I set up for Jesus to take over is connected to *end-of-time* events and will be under the direct control of The Trinity. The marriage of the Lamb comes, and His wife had made herself ready (Revelation 19:7).

## Spiritual Incidents Involving Marriage

Earlier in this chapter, I described a very significant marriage connection. It is the fulfillment of a dream I had of, *"bride and groom coming out of the sea"* – fulfilled through a sermon about *"The Next Great Move of God,"* being *"A Church Without Walls."* I have observed many other spiritual incidents involving marriage.

In 2010, I carried out my second attempt at a divorce after I realized God wanted me to do it. The day before the divorce, He gave my sister a dream to lend me her white dress to wear. After the divorce was complete, by Divine incident, God signal His approval to me. While dressed in white, I got a ride home in a white car and soon after it left the parking lot of the courthouse we came to an intersection. At the intersection, there were four white cars simultaneously positioned in the form of a cross. I had never seen anything like this before.

The next marriage-related incident is that on the day of the dedication of Works Of Trinity, LLC (March 19, 2011), one of the guests who had helped to prepare the office had to go to a wedding in the morning. He left that wedding directly and, still dressed in his wedding clothes, came to the dedication. I did not know about his plan to attend a wedding when I set the date of the dedication, but he did not want to disappoint me by not coming. This is how God made Divine connection of marriage to His company's dedication.

Here is another marriage-related incident. On August 27, 2011 New York and New Jersey were under watch for hurricane, Irene. This was an unusual occurrence, since as far as I can remember, these states wouldn't normally experience hurricanes. Mandatory evacuations were ordered in some parts of each state. I had a 6:00 a.m. flight out of La Guardia Airport, New York to Atlanta, Georgia. I was going to a wedding in the evening and had an early flight that would give me plenty of time to prepare for the wedding. My flight was the only one allowed to leave New York that day. After I left New York, the hurricane hit. God allowed me to leave for a wedding ahead of this disaster.

Here is the last in the series of marriage-related incidents. On October 29, 2011 my cousin was getting married in Long Island, New York, in the evening. An unusual snowstorm overnight extended into the morning of the wedding. Many tree branches fell in my town and elsewhere. While in my house, I was hearing strange noises outside. It was only when I went outside to shovel snow that I realized the noises were due to falling branches.

The snowstorm ended in time for me to go to the wedding. On my way to the wedding, I took the exit off the highway near my house. I was surprised to come upon a large tree branch that fell across the road. It fell in such a way that it formed an archway which I was able to drive through. I later made connection with this incident and the archway at the wedding, which was surrounded with flowers and branches.

The snowstorm was historical for the time of the year; on the day I was attending a wedding. It reminded me of the historical hurricane that came to the tri-state area when I was going to Georgia to attend a wedding. It was the unusual snowstorm on the day I was attending a wedding that caused me to realize that there was something Divinely spiritual going on with weddings and me. It allowed me to make connection to other marriage-related spiritual incidents and the business God has directed me to incorporate for Him. These Divine spiritual incidents suggest that Works Of Trinity, LLC identifies with Jesus' bride, in ways which I don't understand. The Bible is clear that the great city, the holy Jerusalem will come directly out of Heaven from God. It was shown to John as the bride of the Lamb (Revelation 21: 9-27) and was referred to as the tabernacle of God.

*Chapter 3*

# Is Corporate God a New Concept?

You might think that God has nothing to do with commercial business. If so, you are not alone. I was surprised when I realized God wanted me to go into commercial business for Him. After I decided to write this book, I wondered if there were others who God gave the commission to conduct commercial business on His behalf, not counting churches and gospel ministries.

I searched the internet for the words, "*God in business*" and found the book, *God Is at Work: Transforming People and Nations Through Business*, by Ken Eldred. As noted by David Yonggi Cho in Eldred, Christian faith and commerce through teaching the gospel of Jesus can result in profitable business. This is a way of serving God and people in the marketplace. As he also pointed out, God calls some people to work in business the same way He calls others to work in the church. There is spiritual value in God-related business work that can result in the transformation of individuals, society, and nations. Business is another way of advancing the work of the church, globally (Eldred).

God directed me to discover an example of an unusual business, somewhat comparable to Works Of Trinity. On December 29, 2010, I made the unusual decision to sit in front of the TV and eat dinner. I felt I should watch channel 7 since it was just after 6:00 pm and I knew the local news would still be on. I pressed the number 7 on the remote control, but the channel did not change. I pressed 7 again and this time the channel changed.

An interview was taking place. The man being interviewed was talking about using flags with Divinely inspired symbols to worship God in dance and drama. His organization's goal was to enhance the level of worship in churches. The organization is called Gateway to Glory and its name was Divinely inspired. At the end of the interview, I realized by spiritual incident, I was tuned in to channel 77 instead of channel 7. This spiritual movement of enhanced worship of God was only a few towns away from me. God is certainly building up His army of soldiers and making Divine connection to bring them together.

Is there a Godly role that corporate businesses can perform? We read that in Biblical days, God asked people to bring tithe of crop, wine, oil, or animal, which their properties produced for the year, to the place where they worshiped Him. They should eat the tithe at the place of worship and learn to fear God, always. If the place of worship was too far from where people lived; they should sell their products to get money, buy whatever they wanted to eat and drink with the money, and partake of the meal in the house of worship. People should also remember the poor who did not have property to produce crops and animals. Every three years people should bring tithe of what their properties produced to their towns so that those in their communities who did not have – poor, stranger, fatherless, and widow could partake of it. The Lord (God) would bless those who did this (Deuteronomy, 14:22-27).

Business can be a vehicle in aiding those who are less fortunate and as a result reap the blessings of God. You give to God when you give to the poor and needy. Works Of Trinity, LLC was established as God's way of turning around my experiences with spiritual afflictions to help those who are going through similar experiences. God also wants to richly bless me for accomplishing His mission – overcoming spiritual wickedness through the help of the Trinity (God, Jesus, and The Holy Spirit). God's way of turning evil into good is not new. When God redeemed

Jacob and saved him from his enemy, the nation of Israel would rejoice with singing as they receive God's gift of wheat, wine, oil, and animals. They would rejoice with dancing for God would turn their mourning into joy (Jeremiah, 31:11-13).

As an overcomer and one who has been redeemed, I will be taking people into the era of rejoicing and praising God for what He is about to do in commerce. We are certainly living in the *"time of trouble,"* which was predicted in the Bible. It speaks of a *"time of trouble"* which will be the worst in the history of the earth. People whose names are written in God's book will be delivered. Many who were dead will live again. Some will have eternal life while others will suffer eternal shame. Those who are wise will shine as the brightness of the sky and those who teach others what is right will shine as the stars forever (Daniel 12:1-3).

The symbol of Works Of Trinity was chosen as a star by God to reflect the kind of work He is about to do for the world, as we live through this *"time of trouble"* of which the Bible speaks. Economic trouble is the center of many other troubles people are facing. A unique way of spreading the gospel is to help solve economic problems while doing God's work. Going into commercial business for God will alleviate some of the issues related to the dependency on charitable donations to carry out His work. Although I am not the only one called for God's business mission, the story of my calling is unique. This book tells the story of how God called me to do business on His behalf.

Chapter 4
# Finding A Business Name

What's in a name? When people try to name businesses, they often chose names that say something about the expertise, value, or uniqueness of the product and services they offer. In coming up with a name for God's company, I did not have to stress myself to consider if it was the right or wrong name. It was chosen by God Himself.

The vision of the name, Works Of Trinity, was first given in a dream with the abbreviation – WOT. In this dream, *I found myself joining a long line of co-workers who were lining up to leave the company. I got out of the line and later found myself driving to work. At a cross-road, I looked to the left and saw the building of the new place where I was going to work. It had the word, "WOT" written on it.*

Ironically, at the time of this dream I was working on a project called, *"WAN Outage Testing."* It was referred to as, *"WOT"* (Reid---"God Works Through Dreams"). God made sure I would never forget this abbreviation. The project was the seed He planted in me that allowed me to be aware of His choice for His business name.

Later, with the reality of spiritual attacks and the Trinity (God, Jesus, and the Holy Spirit) as my defense (Reid---"God's Mission"). I knew I had to incorporate them into the name of God's company. Recalling the dream about WOT and seeing how the Trinity *"works"* to free me from demonic attacks and intrusion, I came up with two possible names – *"Wonders Of the Trinity"* and *"Works Of Trinity."* I chose to expand the abbreviation, *"WOT,"* to *"Works Of Trinity"* since it fits it exactly without any extra word.

It is usual to first have a name and then form the abbreviation. However backwards this seems – WOT expanded to Works Of Trinity, it is the true story of how the name of God's business was formed. God does not work the same way as human beings. His ways might seem odd to us. I am waiting on God for the day when I can separate myself from my current employer and truly go to work for Works Of Trinity, LLC. He gave me a dream with an idea of when this would occur.

In the process of writing this chapter, I recalled a dream I had on October 11, 2010. In this dream, *I was lying* on my back in bed when I felt the weight of something being placed on my stomach. I knew it was God Who was doing it. I started to hear people talking. Someone clearly said, "It is December 31st." I thought the person meant it would be the last day on my current job.

I next saw a lady at my room door. She started writing on it while I watched from the bed. While still in bed, I also knew I was beside the lady watching her as she wrote on the door. She wrote, "God, Son," and I knew she would also write "Holy Spirit." I started to think, "I will tell Razan, I am leaving the job to work for my God." Razan is my co-worker.

The first dream about leaving my job occurred during a period of uncertainty in which the company was cutting back on workers. It indicated that I would leave on my own. The second dream about leaving my job seems to set a date without a year. However, I know our date and God's date is not the same. Therefore, I do not know when this date will become a reality. When this time comes, I know the true meaning of God's company name will be revealed; as the Trinity conduct their works and allow me to publish their stories.

*Chapter 5*

# The Colors of God's Business

Each color has its symbolic meaning. Therefore, the color for a business should be carefully chosen to enhance the company's image. I did not have to choose the colors of God's business. Like the name of His business, God chose His colors. How God directed me to the colors He chose to represent His business is a little story within itself. The color *"red"* in God's business logo represents the *"blood"* of Jesus Christ, life, and spiritual warfare (conducted through The Holy Spirit). God carefully led me to this color by using many spiritual incidents.

The first spiritual incident leading to the color of God's business was in June 2010. A guest pastor at my church told the congregation they should dress well and look good for God. She next singled out a member of the church and commented on how she was looking good the previous Sunday, in a *"red"* dress. After church, I checked my sister's selection of clothing she was about to give to the Salvation Army and got many clothes in excellent condition, including three *"red"* dresses. I was led to make spiritual connection to the pastor's sermon about dressing good and *"the woman looking good in a red dress."*

On August 28, 2010, I took my daughter shopping for a used car. She indicated that she preferred a "red" car. Two days later, as I continued to shop for a used car, I ended up trading my leased car for a new, leased *"red"* Nissan Versa, even though I started out looking for a used car.

Later at home, there was a spiritual incident in which I went to place the papers for the newly leased *"red"* car at exactly where I had the paid receipt of my previously own Nissan Quest van. It was paid off in 2002 and the first thing that caught my eyes when I picked up the paid receipt was the words, *"PAID IN FULL."* This spiritual incident caused me to remember a dream I had on July 20, 2010. In this dream, I realized God had taken control of my car. He had certain controlled situation such that I ended up with a *"red"* car. He also linked this new car to the van that I had to give away while going through spiritual attacks.

Could it be that God loves Nissan vehicles? When it was close to time for me to return the leased Nissan Versa, God was again in control of the deal. I got a mailed advertisement from the Nissan dealer I had dealt with before. There was the possibility of winning a car, so I decided to check it out. I did not win; neither did I buy a car. However, God led me to another Nissan dealer to check around. There, He controlled every situation such that I bought another Nissan Versa at the price of $22,000, when everything was added in. This reminded me of the *"PAID IN FULL"* receipt I had for my previously owned Nissan Quest which was also priced at exactly $22,000.

Unlike the Nissan Quest, this car caused much drama. From the moment I went into the car, one little thing after the other went wrong, such as low tire pressure indication and turn signal not functioning. Although things were fixed, I started having a very strong feeling that I should return the car, but the dealer would not take it back. I made several trips back and forth to the dealer to persuade the management to take back the car. At one point, the Holy Spirit arose in me and allowed me to tell a few managers, *"God will deal with it."*

The very short version of the drama is that, God allowed me to tell the managers at the dealership about Him taking prescription business from one pharmaceutical company that did not sell books about Him and rewarding another, CVS Pharmacy, for selling books about Him; and that He had led me to His name, Adonai – the Master of everything. Finally, God led me to write Nissan manufacturer and to mention the CVS story and His name, Adonai. After I did this, God released me from the pressing desire to return the car; and I kept it. He wanted to introduce Himself to Nissan and the letter I wrote to the company accomplished this. I am not sure of what future business dealing God has planned with Nissan; I only know that He does not conduct business the same way humans would.

A *"red"* car was not the only *"red"* thing to which God led me. On September 2, 2010, my pull-string lawn mower was giving trouble. My daughter, Sonia, decided that we should get an electrical mower instead of a gas one. She went online and found a hardware store that was having sales on a brand electrical mower. We went to the hardware store and saw the last one on sale. We looked at other brands of electrical mower but decided they were too expensive. We ended up buying the last one on sale.

When we returned home it was late in the night, but I took the time to assemble the mower since Sonia promised she would mow the lawn the next day. The next day, while at work, Sonia called to tell me that when she was about to use the lawn mower she saw that a wheel was broken. I did not notice this when I was assembling it, which was unusual. I returned it to the hardware store. However, since it was the last one in stock, the store manager gave me a different brand to replace it. This new lawn mower was *"red"* instead of gray, like the one I had originally purchased.

God continued to show me *"red."* On September 5, 2010, during the Women's Fellowship service at my church, the president said she would be allowing other women to partake in conducting services. She said her theme was, *"Women of Many Colors"* and explained that the theme referred to the many experiences of women.

After church, I decided to stop by Ruth and borrow her saw to cut a few branches on my property. The color of the saw was *"red."* Within a short space of time – August 29, 2010 to September 5, 2010 – I noticed I was suddenly accumulating *"red"* things. I had *"red"* dresses, *"red"* car, *"red"* lawn mower, and now *"red"* saw. After hearing the Women's Fellowship theme in church and immediately getting the third piece of *"red"* machine, after church; I realized God was assigning the color *"red"* to me. Red was not my favorite color. However, I accepted it because I saw where God was pointing out to me that my color was *"red."*

God is always faithful to confirm my understanding of what He is putting in my spirit. The theme for the Ladies Convention at my church was "*Women of Colors*" – experiences of women relating to God. Since I knew God was pointing me to the color "*red*," during the Ladies Convention on October 16, 2010, as part of my exhortation of Him, I mentioned the many spiritual incidents in my life that indicated my color was "*red*." Before the convention ended, the president of the Ladies Ministry called me to the podium and announced that The Holy Spirit told her to confirm that the color for me was "*red*;" that it meant I was armed and dangerous and no one could touch me without asking God's permission. With this Divine message, I knew I must incorporate the color "*red*" in the design of the logo for Works Of Trinity – God's company.

I later realized that "*red*" was not the only color God has chosen for me. Gold is the other color; and that too has its own story. God used a sequence of spiritual incidents to lead me to incorporating gold into the design of His company's logo and website. It all started when my daughter, Sonia, asked if she could paint her room. It then came to my thought that I should also paint my room. It was at a time when I was wearing gold nail polish after

God led me to wear that color for Easter Sunday, April 8, 2012.

After having thoughts of painting my room in gold, the next day on my way from work I suddenly noticed a house with its railings painted in gold. I had been traveling this route for a few years but did not notice this before. The way I was drawn to take notice of the golden railings was confirmation to me that God wanted me to paint my room in gold.

On this same journey home, I had to meet someone at the shopping mall. Since I was early in meeting him, I stopped at Panera Bread and bought something to eat. When I got up to leave, I noticed that area where I sat was painted in gold with red trimming. That gave me the idea of not only to paint my room in gold but to also trim the doors and windows in red. I hired someone to paint my room and trim it in red. Based on input from my niece and daughter, I painted the ceiling in golden circles. Before my painting project ended, on August 13, 2012, I had a dream that indicated to me why God had me painting golden circles.

In the dreamt, *I was in the basement of a house. I heard the thundering of hoofs. I saw myself as a little person, hanging onto the ceiling as I watched through the windows. I saw a large amount of horses' feet as they ran straight into the upper level of the building. After the thundering of horses' hoofs stopped, I came down the ceiling.*

*A crowd of unusually tall and stately white men and women in uniform were standing at the wall against the window where I had seen the horses' feet. I knew they had come on the horses. I saw another fair-skinned woman and three babies lying on the floor, in the basement where I was.*

This dream really brought out the majestic meaning of the color "*gold*" and speaks to the revelation of Jesus' second coming to earth, written about in Revelation 19. Preceded with thundering announcement of the wedding of the Lamb and His bride; Jesus Christ (The Lamb) with eyes like flame of fire and wearing many crowns, appeared on a white horse. The stately men and women in uniform, riding horses, in the dream, represent the armies in white, clean clothing that followed Jesus. Jesus is called *"Faithful and True."* He will come to judge in righteousness and to make war. In the revelation to John, Jesus has a name written that no one except himself knew. His clothing is bloody, and He is called, *"The Word of God."* He has a sharp sword in His mouth to defeat the nations. He will rule over them with a rod of iron. He will trample the winepress and show them the furious anger of The Almighty God. His clothing and thigh has the name written: *"King of Kings, and Lord of Lords"* (Revelation 19:4-16).

There are other symbolic meanings of gold, such as purification and trial by fire, riches, deity, holiness, majesty (Revelation 3:18; 4:4; Malachi 3:3); trial of faith, praise, honor, and glory at the appearing of Jesus Christ (1 Peter 1:7). However, the majestic return of Jesus is what God led me to emphasize.

My gold and red painting project ended with God further acknowledging my obedience in following His guidance. I helped to finish the painting but suffered the consequence of aggravating my back, especially in the hip area. To ease the pain, I took two painkillers and then laid down on my back to rest. As I tried to relax, I played MSM Monthly CD Teaching by Matt Sorger – *Sustaining A Permanent Change*. The scripture reading was from Genesis 32:24-32. It was the story of Jacob wrestling with an angel until the angel blessed him. However, the angel had put Jacob's hip out of joint during the wrestling (Sorger---"Sustaining A Permanent Change"). As I heard about the hip being out of joint, my spirit groaned in acknowledgement of my situation and my leg with the hip problem made up and down movements, a few times.

God used Matt Sorger's message to acknowledge what I had accomplished. Until I heard the message and saw my reaction to Jacob's hip problem, I did not know that God had challenged me to accomplish the painting task He had given me, even though I had met in a car accident after I had started it. I was determined to follow God's direction in painting my room in gold and red.

Through constant aggravation of my back problems, I completed the task with help, only to eventually have the time to sit and listen to this relevant message of hip problem. To add to this, I fell asleep while listening to the sermon, but woke up in time to hear Matt said, *"I lay my life on the altar..."* I also made connection with this part of the message. Prior to listening to this CD, on August 7, 2012, I had gone to the police precinct where my car accident occurred, to collect a police report form. I then stopped by my church's Ladies Ministry meeting where I laid on the altar and asked the ladies to pray for me. I did not let them know that I had made up my mind to give up my body to God at the altar because of my injuries from the accident.

After seeing the way God led me to the color, *"gold,"* I decided to replace *"black"* in His company's logo with "*gold*." It was not only His logo that God wanted me to use "*red*" and "*gold*" colors, but also on His website.

On November 27, 2012, while I was in the process of getting God's website built, I had a dream that directed me as to how the banner should look. I dreamt, *I was outside a building. One of my co-workers was there. I looked towards the sky and saw a large burning flame of gold against the blue sky. I thought, "The sky is burning."*

*I took my phone camera and started taking pictures. I thought to myself, "I have to send these to my website designer." After taking the pictures, I sent them to my website designer from my phone. I could see the message lines on the phone.*

After I woke up from this dream, I soon heard a message beep on my phone. I checked and saw it was a message from my website designer to check the website. I saw that he had changed the banner to a picture with flaming gold colors in most areas and blue intermingled within it. I knew God was showing me that this is the banner He had selected. The website designer had been trying different colors.

The use of the color "*red*" and "*gold*" in God's business identify – logo and website, is indicative of the blood of Jesus Christ and His majesty. As indicated in the book of Revelation 19:11-16, He will be coming back to earth, riding a white horse, having his garment stained with blood, wearing many crowns, and will be followed by a stately army, dressed in clean white clothing.

*Chapter 6*
# The Display of God's Color

I previously described the display of God's colors in terms of the spiritual experiences He allowed me to have. The theme for our 2010 Ladies' Convention was *"Women of Many Colors"* and this referred to the experiences of the women. After the president of the Ladies' Ministry at my church confirmed God had assigned the color *"red"* to me, He demonstrated the meaning of that color. The following day, October 17, 2010, was the last day of the 3-day Ladies' Convention. There the Holy Spirit went into action, through me – demonstrating the color of God's business.

A woman who spoke to my bishop on his radio program came to church for prayer to get rid of demonic spirits she knew were trying to destroy her life. Near the close of the main service, my bishop called the woman to pray for her. He put on a gospel selection to play. As my bishop spoke to her, he anointed her with Olive oil and gave the oil to a church member to pour into the hands of other members so that they could help to pray for the woman.

One church member got some oil in her hands and rubbed some on mine. I next began to rub the oil together in both of my hands, vigorously. This was an indication that the Holy Spirit took control of me and allowed me to enter spiritual warfare to help free the woman from demons. My eyes were closed as I made movements directed by the Holy Spirit. After a while, my bishop detected that some of the demonic spirits had left the woman. The Holy Spirit within me ended the fight.

Everyone in the church was amazed. A few other church members and my cousin, Lea, who I had invited to church, had also entered spiritual warfare on behalf of the woman. While I rested from battle, others were still engaged, under the direction of the Holy Spirit within them.

Very soon, Lea, detected that the demon, which was cast out from the first woman went into another woman. Other church members and my bishop rallied around her until they were able to help her get rid of the demon that entered her.

My bishop explained that a demon will enter the weakest person it can find. Since this woman was grieving from the recent loss of her father and was tired, she was weak enough to be the victim.

This spiritual battle demonstrated that God's had given me the power to cast out demons; I was armed and dangerous, spiritually; and anyone would have to go through Him to get to me. It was my first public battle and the first time I had to defend someone. I have had many spiritual battles where the Holy Spirit directed me in defending myself against spiritual attacks. This spiritual battle demonstrated that people who are oppressed, suppressed, and sickened by evil and demonic spirits can get delivered by Divine spiritual warriors, working to free them through the power of the Trinity – God, Jesus, and The Holy Spirit.

The Holy Spirit of God continued to demonstrate the color of His business in public, when I least expected it. As according to what He allowed me to type in the company's Operating Agreement, activities of His company will be as authorized by the Trinity. Therefore, He chooses when and how I use the power He has given me to conduct His business.

My second public spiritual battle was to defend a visiting bishop at my church. He was having a series of meetings in New York and surrounding states, which were successful and caused envy among a few pastors in the community. This guest bishop started a series of meetings at my church from June 4, 2011 to June 10, 2011. Although the word meeting is used, it was church service outside of normal scheduled Sunday worship. Even though I was working late each day at my job, I decided to attend all the meetings because I knew in my spirit that God wanted me to be there. I do not typically attend any meetings unless I know God wants me to be there since I travel from another State, which is far from my church. This guest bishop was a very powerful preacher and I could see why people would want to hear him preach.

At the end of the series of meetings on Friday June 10, 2011, when I was the most tired, I realized why God wanted me to attend them all. This meeting was running much later than the previous ones. It went on to the next day. I was thinking of walking out because I knew I had to go to work later in the morning and would not get enough sleep. However, I stayed because I did not want to be rude. After the guest bishop ended his sermon my bishop took over. He started prophesying to the congregation.

Later, my bishop said he would count to seven and the congregation should shout, *"Halleluiah,"* as he counted. In the middle of doing so, my bishop said he heard an organ in the atmosphere. He stopped the counting and said we should wait for the musician. The organist found the background music my bishop said he was hearing. He said there were five persons with businesses who should come to the altar. He also said that we should bring our house keys to the altar. I got my house key and went to stand at the altar.

My bishop continued to prophesy to the congregation. The Holy Spirit then revealed to him that there were five people in the community, including three women, who came together to discuss the guest bishop. These people thought the guest bishop was expanding too rapidly. One woman said she was jealous and it should have been her. After a while, my bishop asked everybody to pray for the guest bishop. During the prayer, The Holy Spirit revealed to my bishop that there was an old chariot with horses of demons outside the church, waiting to attack the guest bishop and kill him. The five people who were against him had sent them.

As I heard my bishop spoke of the chariot of demons, I let out a warfare cry as I went into battle on behalf of the guest bishop, by the power of The Holy Spirit. My eyes were closed. I positioned my left hand out with a fist and my right hand across my chest in a fist. I waited as my bishop continued to talk, and described the chariot and the demons within it. He started to speak to the demons and as he spoke, I made various warfare movements. The Holy Spirit allowed my bishop to speak in French, German, and English, even though he only knew English and Jamaican dialect.

At the end of the warfare, when my bishop told the demons to die, my final action was to fall at the altar in front of the guest bishop. I laid there on my stomach for a while. This was a demonstration that God gave me the power to kill demons. During a period of continuous brutal spiritual attacks, God has previously anointed me to kill demons (Reid---"God's Mission").

The third public display of the color of God's business occurred on August 7, 2011, at my church. As usual, the Holy Spirit initiated it. Before this took place, it seemed that my spirit knew something honorable was going to happen to me. At the beginning of the service, the first song the moderator requested to be sung was one she said came to her spirit to sing at church. It was two verses of a hymn. I was very pleased when she announced a familiar hymn we used to sing at the church I grew up in.

The first verse of the hymn is: *Pass me not, O gentle Savior; hear my humble cry; while on others Thou art calling; do not pass me by.* The chorus is: *Savior, Savior, Hear my humble cry; while on others Thou art calling; do not pass me by.* As the congregation sang, I was overwhelmed in my spirit. I started to cry. I was not sure if it was due to the familiarity of the song and the memory it brought back. In that moment, I recalled the dream I had the previous night about *being at the church I grew up in and was looking for two verses in the Bible to give a man to sing at the pulpit.*

Exodus 15:1-15 was the scripture read in church. My spirit was stirred to tears again when verses 1 and 2 were read. Verse 1 reads: *Then sang Moses and the children of Israel this song unto the Lord, and spake, saying, I will sing unto the Lord, for He hath triumphed gloriously; the horse and his rider hath He thrown into the sea.* Verse 2 reads: *The Lord is my strength and song, and He is become my salvation. He is my God, and I will prepare him a habitation. My father's God and I will exalt him.*

I could relate to this song Moses and the children of Israel were singing because God has brought me through some very brutal spiritual attacks. I lived to write about them and to go into business for God, based on these experiences. I had also prepared a business office for God, in my basement. After dedicating His office, every time I enter in, I would feel His presence and I realize God is truly occupying His office, ready to direct His business. This continued for a few weeks, as God's acknowledgement of what I had done for Him.

After the reading of the scripture about Moses and the children of Israel, a few members in the church started rebuking evil spirits, in the name of Jesus. It was usual of these church members to detect when someone enters the church with evil spirits. After a while, they calmed down and the service continued.

Later in church, I noticed a woman wearing a red dress that was like the one I have and had labeled as *"The Holy Spirit dress."* It was the third red dress I wore after God arranged for me to have some clothes from my sister, Petra, and it was the one in which I did my first public spiritual battle. The woman introduced herself during the welcome session. She said she heard my bishop on the radio and decided to visit his church.

Sometime after, my bishop took over the service. He called the woman to pray for her. My bishop was asking God why he was giving him that task to do. He said God asked him to untie this woman and send back the evil to the woman who placed it on her to kill her. This would enable the woman to live and not die. He asked each sides of the congregation to repeat *"warfare"* for a while before he started praying for the woman.

At one point in the prayer, my bishop said that he could see the woman who set the evil spirit on the woman for whom he was praying. This woman was wearing a red headband that was red and white. I was wearing a red headband and red and white scrunches. As if this description of the woman was my queue to go into spiritual battle, I let out *"the battle cry"* and positioned my left hand outstretch in a fist and my right hand underneath it, in a fist.

I was positioned that way for a while until The Holy Spirit moved me to make other spiritual movements. At one point, I find myself beating the floor with my two fists and then slapping it with the palm of both my hands. Throughout the battle, I had my eyes closed, which was what I came to accept as the norm whenever I go into spiritual battle for someone.

After the warfare ended and I opened my eyes, I saw the woman, on whose behalf I was battling, lying stretched out on the floor on her back. A white sheet was covering her from her chest down. It was usual for a church member to cover a woman as she enters spiritual warfare, to prevent exposure while fighting. At the end of the battle, I hugged the woman as she thanked me.

My bishop later explained to the congregation that when I had my hand outstretched in a fist, I was sending an arrow to the woman who set evil spirit on the woman for whom he was praying. He further explained that when I was beating the floor I was opening the grave where the woman's spirit was buried. The Holy Spirit took my spirit down in the grave and freed the woman's spirit. I then placed the spirit of the wicked woman in the grave, hence returning the evil she did to the woman on whose behalf I was doing spiritual battle.

Later my bishop anointed me and prayed for me. I found myself, crying out, *"Yes"* vigorously three times as my bishop spoke of the anointing God has placed on me. He blew on me and said I should receive the breath of God. Later my spirit led me to kneel in reverence to God. This reminded me of the business meeting I had with the Trinity. I was saying, *"Yes Jesus,"* several times.

The act of the bishop blowing on me and telling me to receive the breath of God reminded me of the service at my church on June 14, 2011 in which a visiting prophet spoke with emphasis; and the breath of the words went straight to my mouth, even though I was very far from him.

At that time, I had wondered about the significance of this spiritual incident. The prophet, had read from Luke 4:26, *"But unto none of them was Elias sent, save unto Sarepta, a city of Sidon, unto a woman who was a widow."* He had emphasized the fact that God sent Elias to one woman although there were many there to see Elias. He had mentioned that maybe God sent him to just one woman even though there were many there. I was wondering if I was that one woman since I had felt the breath of his words on my mouth, from very far away.

The third display of the color of God's business was my public anointing. Even though God had anointed me in private when I was going through a series of brutal spiritual battles due to multiple levels of evil and demonic spirits that were sent against me, He wanted others to witness that I am His anointed. After all, if I am going to represent His business to the world, I must be identified, publicly.

On August 11, 2010 during the day, I had some concerns about what I had written and needed reassurance from Jesus Christ that all I had written in this book had His approval. I prayed vigorously for Jesus to confirm what I had written, so that I do not misrepresent Him in any way. I reminded Jesus I was doing it all for Him.

That night, I woke up to a strange noise. I then started to do spiritual movements with my hands that were reflective of past spiritual warfare experiences. I was taken through all the areas of my body that came under attack – my ears, legs, stomach, head, neck, heart, belly, and face. My final body position represented Jesus on the cross. This reminded me of pictures with Jesus on the cross and of a similar body positioning that happened to me while I was going through brutal spiritual attacks (Reid---"God's Mission").

I realized that my awakening experience of repositioning my body to areas I suffered spiritual attacks repeatedly, was an act of Jesus. He had responded to my prayer to let me know I should write about all my experiences with spiritual attacks, just as He had taken me through the movements to remind me of them. He reminded me of personal spiritual attacks and of the spiritual battles, I had fought on behalf of others.

It was Jesus Christ Who asked me to write books for Him, about my experiences. The final positioning of my body to depict the image of Jesus on the cross was confirmation of His approval of what I had written and to identify that it was He Who was responding to my prayers. In effect, it was a sign-off on the contents of His books. This boosted my confidence in representing the color of God's business as, "the blood of Jesus Christ, His Majesty, and spiritual warfare."

*Chapter 7*

# God's Logo for Works Of Trinity

The choice of logo for Works Of Trinity is an interesting story that tells of how God guided me into doing what He desired of me. I will first describe with pictures, the progression of the logo's design before I get into the stories behind the progression.

The progression of the logo design for Works Of Trinity is shown below. God perfected His business' logo, based on the works He predestined for it.

| | |
|---|---|
| 1st draft of logo – by inspiration from battle with the 666 demon.<br><br> | 2nd draft of logo – due to name associated with rare star; God chose this over the cross.<br><br> |
| 1st finalized logo.<br><br> | 2nd finalized logo – redesign due to comments about the Star of David and "*WOT*" abbreviation.<br><br> |

3rd finalized logo – combines previously finalized logos due to an article by John Todd, leading to the revelation of what God is sending me against. In addition, I replaced *"black"* with *"gold"* based on God's color choices.

The design of Works Of Trinity's logo was first inspired by the experience I had with the 666 demon. In this experience, the number 333 was pronounced by my spirit as mine; after declaring that the name of Jesus is mighty and that He rose from the dead on the third day (Reid---"God's Mission"). I therefore, decided to incorporate 333 and the cross in the logo's design. The number 333 symbolizes the Trinity and the death and resurrection of Jesus Christ.

After God confirmed that the color for me was *"red,"* I decided that the logo would have a *"red"* cross to depict the blood of Jesus Christ, which was shed on the cross to redeem people from sin. The first idea of a logo for

Works Of Trinity, therefore, consisted of a *"red"* cross with the number *"333,"* written vertically and horizontally.

I did a rough draft of the logo and submitted it to a designer for review. The person did not like it. I decided this person did not like my logo because he did not understand the meaning of it. Although I respected his opinion, I did not intend to change it. However, it turned out God was speaking through him. The *"red"* and *"333"* part of the logo was correct, but the design was not what God wanted. It is quite a story the way God guided me to change His logo.

On September 20, 2010, I had to rent a car to go to work. While at the car rental business, one of the clerks, of East Indian descent, noticed my name. He told me he had a daughter with the same name, but it was spelt with one *"n."* He then asked me if I knew the meaning of my name. After telling him I did not know, he told me it was the name of a *"rare star."*

In the evening, I decided to search the web for my name as well as the names of stars to see if what the East Indian man told me was true. I spent about one and a half hour searching for a rare star with my name but didn't find it. I concluded that my sister must have gotten my name from our grandmother who was from East Indian ancestry.

Although I did not find a rare star with my name, I found an article about the discovery of a rare star-making galaxy ("Rare star-making galaxy found"). I made a spiritual connection to the unconfirmed meaning of my name to be that of a *"rare star"* and the article on the rare star-making galaxy.

After I went on the internet and used the search engine *"Google"* to find my name, I remembered the warning from the Ladies Ministry president of my church, not to *"Google"* each other's names. This was said after the members randomly chose names of prayer partners, during one of the Ladies' Ministry meeting. I realized that God had used the Ladies' Ministry president to indicate to me that He would be leading me to do a search on my name.

The Holy Spirit of God continued to allow me to make more connection with *"star."* On September 21, 2010, I decided to check out the different pricing category on my home security company's website since my monthly rate should be less, based on my use of fewer sensors than originally assigned. The previous evening, I had contacted the company and programmed the exchanged sensors they sent me. I had recently installed security at my house, after there was a break-in.

Although I had noticed a *"red"* image in the middle of the security company's logo on the yard sign that came with the security package, I did not pay much attention to it. I had even visited the company's website but did not pay attention to its logo either. This time, by spiritual incident, the logo was the first thing I noticed when I visited the company's website. I was surprised to see there was a *"red"* star in the middle of the logo.

Immediately, I felt in my spirit that I should redesign God's logo with a *"red"* star instead of a *"red"* cross. I realized God led me to use this home security provider so that I could make the connection with their logo and the logo He wanted for His company. I was becoming more spiritually attuned to the different incidents that God was using to direct me in creating His logo. I recalled that the expert designer had told me he did not like my first draft of the logo. That evening, I redesigned Works Of Trinity's logo, using a *"red"* star instead of a *"red"* cross. I then told God He had two logos from which to choose.

On September 22, 2010, while at work, I got a usual *"Books 24x7 New Title Notification"* email. I knew it was an alert for new books added to the online book access to which my company subscribes for its employees. I am normally too busy to check out the notifications. This time,

God put it in my spirit to check on this email, even though I was busy. I downloaded the blocked pictures and then made the unusual decision to scroll through the list of books to see reviews of the topics.

I was amazed to see a book with the title, "*SWITCH*" and with a symbol of a star encased in a circle. I realized this was a swift response from God; after asking Him to choose which of the two logos He wanted me to use. The title of the book was clearing telling me to switch to the star logo. Similar to the symbol of the star encased in a circle on this book, the new logo I had designed had a "*red*" star, partially encased in the name, "*Works Of Trinity.*" In addition, I had written the words in the new Works Of Trinity's logo in a circular fashion. By spiritual incidents, God directed me to a "*red*" star that should be a part of His business' logo. He clearly showed His choice of logo when presented with two drafts.

God chose the star and not the cross because the works of the cross had already been accomplished. Jesus Christ came and bore the cross – paying for our sins and paving the way to God, through Him. Now, Jesus will be the shining star that guides me in conducting God's business, as I continue His work for Him. He has been guiding others who trust in Him.

I know the logo God directed me to create has Divine spiritual meaning. It is symbolic of His works on earth. My first finalized design for God's business logo had a 5-sides red star, 333, Works Of Trinity, and its abbreviation, WOT, all encased in double circles. I thought this was the final design, based on the one to which God directed me to switch. However, with more spiritual insights, God directed me to do some refinements to His logo.

On February 6, 2011, some men were at my house to do work. We were discussing the recent incident of my carport being torn down by the weight of ice. I told them something good will come out of this disaster. I said this because I remembered the break-in at my house, which led me to the security company with the red star in its logo. This in turn, led me to the idea of a *"red"* star in God's logo after a man told me that my name was that of a *"rare star."* After telling the men this story, I decided to show them the logo. Immediately one of the men said it was *"The star of David."* I felt in my spirit that the man's comment about *"The star of David"* should not be taken lightly. Therefore, I decided to find out more about it.

In the meantime, another spiritual incident pointed me to the same concern that the logo might not be the final version God wanted. On February 8, 2011, the editor assigned to my book, *God's Mission: Spiritual Battles and Revelation of Anti-666*, called me to discuss my experiences and to get a good feel of how I wanted to present my book. He suggested that I remove the abbreviation *"WOT"* for Works Of Trinity since it would dilute the story I am telling. I did not want people to forget that *"Works Of Trinity"* means that The Trinity (God, Jesus, and the Holy Spirit) were doing works in a might way. I agreed with the editor to remove the *"WOT"* abbreviation and started to seriously think of removing it from the logo.

As it turned out, *"WOT"* abbreviation in God's logo was not the only thing that needed to be changed. On February 11, 2011, I decided to search the internet to see if the star in God's logo truly matches *"The star of David,"* as the man visiting me had said. In the online Wikipedia encyclopedia, I found out it is a hexagram (6-sided) star that is used as a Jewish symbol and represents *"The God of Israel."* It was presented in blue and red. However, *"The Red Star of David"* is Israel's only official emergency medical, disaster, ambulance service.

I knew I had to yet again redesign the logo to make the stars match *"The Star of David."* After all, Jesus said to John, *"I Jesus have sent mine angel to testify unto you these things in the churches. I am the root and the offspring of David, and the bright and morning star"* (Revelation 22:16).

Based on my research on *"The Star of David"* and the comment about *"WOT"* from my editor, I decided to modify God's logo. I removed the abbreviation, *"WOT"* and made all stars 6-sided instead of 5-sided. I told the logo designer to fill the circle with small stars and by spiritual incident, it turned out to be twelve of them. I find this Divine connection to *"The Star of David"* very interesting since the logo has one main star and twelve small red stars, which would represent the twelve tribes of Israel. Jesus also had twelve disciples; it would also fit this model with Jesus as the main star and the twelve disciples as the twelve small stars. Through a series of spiritual incidents, God directed me in creating the logo He wanted for His business.

I felt in my spirit that God's logo has special significance for people originating from Israel and India. There is Divine connection in the fact I was told by a man from India that my name was that of a *"rare star,"* just before discovering the *"red star"* in my security company's logo. My grandmother ancestry is from India. This grandmother married my grandfather who I found out was a half Jew after I was telling my niece about the story of

God's logo and *"The Star of David."* I further made spiritual connection to an employee of the Israeli embassy in the U.S.A. who, innocently, caused an accident involving me. The accident turned out to be a cover for inflicting spiritual attacks on me (Reid---"God's Mission").

After God's logo was finalized for the second time with the true *"Star of David,"* I felt very confident that my work with it was complete. It, therefore, took me by surprise when God led me to a third change. I overheard a conversation about the death of Whitney Houston, which led me to the stories of John Todd and his experiences with witchcraft. He explained that witches use a five-pointed star within a circle and have a six-pointed star within a circle beside it, when practicing witchcraft (Todd).

I immediately realized that God wanted His logo to be also symbolic of the reversal of witchcraft and similar practices. At first, I feared the similarities with what John Todd described and the final logo God was directing me to produce. However, I know I serve The Almighty God, The Creator of Heaven and earth. I have come to realize that Satan tries to imitate God in every way because he thought he could overthrow God and take God's position. I, therefore, stand in obedience to God to make His desired changes to His logo so that the works of Satan can be reversed.

While I was going through very brutal spiritual attacks initiated by individuals who practice witchcraft, I had promised God to help those who were going through similar experiences. I, therefore, made few changes to God's logo. By this time, God had shown me that the color "gold" is also assigned to me. I replaced the *"black"* color with *"gold"* color, combined the two previously "finalized" logos, and connected them so that they are side by side. God allowed me to finalize the first two logos separately so that I would immediately realize that He wanted both to be combined in His *"truly finalized"* logo.

The *"truly finalized"* logo of Works Of Trinity is God's way of arming me to carry out the promise I made to Him to expose and reverse spiritual wickedness, so that people can be delivered from evil and demonic oppression and suppression. The finalized logo also carries with it all the previous meanings attributed to it – Jesus being the main star and His death and resurrection. After all, Jesus will be coming back to rule the earth and fight the 666 demon – the mark of the beast (Revelation 19).

*Chapter 8*

# The Story of This Book Cover

In establishing all aspects of Works Of Trinity, the Trinity constantly makes visible contribution to the formation of the ideas, always in unique ways. The design for this book cover was no exception. My original plan for the book cover was to use the Heavenly background from one of the other books without any special picture in the forefront. As it turned out, God had another plan. His plan came to me in dreams combined with spiritual incidents.

On December 3, 2010, I dreamt, *I was in a church, but it was not the one I usually attend. Al Gore, former Vice President of the United States, was there. I knew he was there to help organize the operation of Works Of Trinity. As I stood around, a large beam of light penetrated my body. I knew it was the light of God. While still in the church, I next find myself laying out a blue dress and blue scarf which I planned to wear.*

*Next, a white lady joined us in the church. I looked around and saw that the benches were now filled with people. The white woman started to speak. She walked down the aisle and I followed behind her. As she walked, she stretched both hands out to the people sitting on either side of the aisle. In the last bench, one of the persons was a woman who had come to my church when she had demons trying to destroy her life.*

*As the white woman stretched her hands across that bench, she went into spiritual warfare. The other woman with the demonic issue got out of the bench and walked out the door. The white woman and I followed her out as the white woman continued in spiritual warfare.*

*Next, I found myself outside the same church. I was walking with Al Gore. We were surveying the property to see where we could make a building for Works Of Trinity. I saw a tall post with the word, 'TRINITY' written vertically. It was in a large hole with white mall on the inside. This indicated to me that work was in progress to build another building. There were two workers near the mall hole.*

*The other part of the land was fenced around and had a large area of bushes. Al Gore said to me, "We should make it four to six o'clock so that it won't interfere with church service." I knew he was talking about activity for Works Of Trinity.*

Taking heed to the dream about blue clothing, on December 5, 2010, the next Sunday, I wore to church, a blue skirt and a darker blue shirt that was the same color as the scarf in the dream. I decided to take my netbook computer with me, so I could show my sister, Ruth, the final logo for Works Of Trinity. I also wanted to show her the progress of the book covers for the other books that I had someone working on. I would have emailed them to her, but she was experiencing network outages with her service provider for almost a week and would not be able to access her email.

A regular part of service at my church is to welcome visitors and greet each other with a hug. On this day, the church member who was called on to greet the visitors said this time we would do it differently. We would tell each other our names. As usual, a song selection was played during the process. This time, the song was played unusually high. I had difficulty hearing the *"name"* of the person I was greeting. I felt discouraged by this. I did not bother to greet some people. I made my way to where my bishop was, at the sound control, and I told him the music was too loud. He turned it down.

## The Story of This Book Cover

During the sermon, the speaker box started to make a knocking sound for a while. My bishop said God was knocking on someone's door. During the church service, my bishop spoke at length about water baptism because he had some candidates for water baptism. This was going to be at another church at 5:00 p.m. since our church did not have a pool. During the sermon, he mentioned that the spirit of the person who baptizes people gets passed on to those they baptize. He gave the example that if he was indulging in witchcraft and was to baptize people then that kind of spirit would get passed on to those he baptizes. Soon after he spoke those words a recent member of the church stood up and said she was in a church two years ago and later found out the pastor who baptized her was dabbling in witchcraft. She said she would like to be baptized again to get rid of that spirit around her.

My bishop invited others to be baptized again, if they wish to do so. One of the board of trustees for the church indicated she wanted to be baptized again. At the end of the sermon, nineteen people raised their hands to indicate they wanted to be baptized.

I must pause here to apologize to The Trinity (God, Jesus Christ, and The Holy Spirit) for attempting to cut back on the details of what I had written, due to constant feedback from a friend and managers at my job that I write with too much detail. I thank The Trinity for Their forgiveness and the opportunity to revert to what I had previously written; also, to include this apology and the story of how I was Divinely chastised. On September 21, 2015, while doing what I thought was the final review of this book's manuscript, I decided to cut out the details of the above two paragraphs which speaks of baptism. God knew I was doing this because of the many feedbacks I had in the past of *"too much detail"* in my writing. I felt a very strong disturbance in my spirit as I picked up my laptop to continue editing the manuscript. I realized that God wanted me to stop what I was doing. I closed my laptop and prayed for Divine instruction on how to proceed.

I fell asleep. I dreamt, *I was lying on my bed, on my back. There was also two of me standing at the foot of the bed. One of me, who was standing said, "How comes there is three of me." One of me moved to the other who was lying on the bed and started hitting me in the head.*

After I woke up, I asked God to forgive me of my sin for putting the opinions of others before His instructions. He had shown me as three persons with one fighting the other. As I laid down and contemplated on what just happened, God had me moving my right hand across my belly while I repeated the word, *"important,"* for about three minutes, continuously. The Holy Spirit next spoke out, through me, *"Everything I experience is important."* God then placed it in my spirit that there are many people in the situation of the woman who needed to be baptized again because of being baptized by someone working witchcraft. God indicated that everything He allowed me to experience, to observe, and to write about is important to Him. The details are needed in His stories. What is important to my God (Adonai) is also important to me. He knows what it takes to accomplish His works.

Instead of taking away the details from God's story, I had to add an apology to it. I realized God wants me to be focused, like an eagle, on His works and not be distracted by the opinions of or feedbacks from others. I did not think I needed detail description; however, my Almighty Creator knows me far better than I know yourself, and He also knows His intended audience. He knows that the detail is needed. I stand in obedience to Him.

I will never forget the awakening to dream and back to awakening chastisement from God, about feedbacks from others. After this chastisement, the following Sunday I gave a very short testimony at my church about the name, Adonai, by which God had indicated I should call Him. The guest preacher commented about my testimony; that I should not be speaking about the name of God if I was not giving enough explanation, otherwise I would confuse the congregation. He did not know that I have been constantly giving short testimonies about the name, Adonai, as I walk in obedience to God. After his preaching ended, I spoke to him and tell him a little bit about my experiences with God. After his comment, I had realized that God used him to test me, for me to demonstrate if I had learned from His chastisement of me about paying attention to others' feedbacks and not following His instructions. I told the guest preacher that I have had many experiences with God and God had told me that they are all important to Him. After this important interruption, I will now return to God's baptismal story.

After church was over, I went to Ruth's house and showed her the draft book covers on my netbook. Although I didn't feel like going to the water baptism later, I decided to go since I had expected God to show me something. I knew He had pointed me to wearing the blue dress for a reason. That reason was not clear to me yet. I did not even experience the light of God absorbing my body as I thought it would, according to the dream. I decided maybe God would show me something at the baptism.

The baptism was performed by the bishop of my church with the assistance of the pastor of the church we were using. The children were baptized first. One of them caught my attention. While she was in the pool, my bishop asked her *"name,"* as he had done for the others. I heard my bishop said, *"There are many stars in the sky, but we have one here on earth with us."* He said the little girl's *"name"* was, *Star."*

Immediately I recalled that I wore the blue clothing to church because of what was indicated in the dream. I had shown Ruth the original draft of my book covers, which featured blue sky, white clouds, the moon, and many stars in the background. At church earlier, we were told to tell each other our names, but I was unable to hear most of the names. God knew I did not like loud music and it would catch my attention. I realized it was His way of telling me to pay attention to *"name."*

I recalled the dream with the pole having, *"TRINITY"* written vertically on it. The pole was upright in a hole with white mall in it and two workers were standing by. It became clear to me that the scene in the dream was the baptismal pool I was looking at, which was painted white on the inside, and the two workers were my bishop and the pastor who was assisting him.

While another little girl was in the pool, my bishop spoke that, *"We have a Mariah, but not Mariah Carey."* I also paid attention to this *"name."* His comment caused me to reflect on a dream I had about me singing with Mariah Carey. I know God has a plan to draw her to Him. This baptism with Mariah Carey's *"name"* being called was confirmation of God's plan for her. My dream of her led me to write a chapter about God's call for Mariah Carey, *"An Existing Star Is Called."*

After my bishop was finished baptizing the children, he started with the adults. Soon after the church member who was on the board of trustee stepped into the water, The Holy Spirit took control of her. After she settled down, my bishop declared that God had troubled the water. I was able to make the connection between the level of authority this church member (a board member) had and Al Gore (former Vice President of the United States) in my dream about Works Of Trinity on December 3, 2010. I also realized that the light of God I experienced in the dream penetrating my body was The Holy Spirit penetrating this church member's body.

In the baptismal ceremony, God demonstrated water baptism and Holy Spirit baptism. The baptism of John – The Baptist, is with water to show that we are repenting from our sin, seeking forgiveness of sins and accepting Jesus Christ; but the baptism of Jesus Christ is with The Holy Spirit and fire (Matthew 3:11; Mark 1:4-8; Luke 3:3, 3:16; John 1:26-33; Acts 13:14, 19:4). When we get baptized, we are partaking in the death of Jesus Christ. We go under the water as when He was buried and raised from the water as when He rose from the dead by the glorious power of God – The Father. After baptism, we live new lives with Jesus (Romans 6:4). It is God's wish that we accept Jesus Christ as our savior and be baptized.

I thought about the spiritual incidents surrounding the baptism – the dream of me wearing blue dress and the TRINITY pole in a large hole, representing a baptismal pool. I then became aware that God was directing me to incorporate the act of water baptism on this book cover. The book cover shows the baptism of a rare star declaring her commitment to God, submerging in the baptismal water, rising in newness with God, and being proclaimed as a child of God. The act of water baptism on this book cover is a symbol of: a) spiritual newness in life as we repent from sin and walk with Jesus; and b) The Trinity (God, Jesus, and The Holy Spirit) going into the business of saving souls.

*Chapter 9*

# The Marketing Environment

In establishing His business, God directed me, through spiritual incidents, to His choice of logo and key business partners – a web service provider for His website, a printer for His books, and a Merchant Account provider to sell His books and other products. Later, when I opened a business account at my credit union, by spiritual incident, the savings account showed a negative value in *"red,"* even though money was supposed to be transferred into the business account. I recognized this as a signature of God's approval, using my assigned color. The account issue was later corrected.

As the head of all businesses, God did not forget about advertisement. He had set the stage for the launch of His business. News such as UFO sightings and witchcraft in politics have paved the way for people to pay attention to information about spiritual interferences in their lives and for them to receive the healing and spiritual enlightenment

God's business will bring to the world. News of UFO sightings alerted the public to the existence of other beings that can influence our existence. News of witchcraft association with a politician served to open the eyes of the public to the real existence of spiritual wickedness, even in high places ("US politician dabbled in witchcraft, tape reveals").

According to Morningstar, on September 27, 2010, the National Press Club Conference *"UFO's & Nukes"* took place in Washington. Robert Hastings did a presentation on repeated UFO intrusions into USAF nuclear facilities during the past several decades. The witnesses he cited were credible professionals. They were able to give *"unique and detailed personal accounts of UFOs incidents, in which flying saucers were observed monitoring and, in some cases, tampering with nuclear-tipped ballistic missiles"* in several bases across the United States (Morningstar). With this news item, people will be more receptive to hearing about spiritual interferences in human's activities and their physical and mental well-being.

A September 2010 news article from Deccan Chronicle On The Web reported that Christine O'Donnell, the Republican nominee from Delaware, admitted on the

"*Politically Incorrect*" television show that she had dabbled in witchcraft ("US politician dabbled in witchcraft, tape reveals"). This news item helped to open the eyes of the public to the existence of spiritual evil in the form of witchcraft, voodoo, obeah, Santa Maria, and other names by which such acts are known.

The anti-venom for spiritual afflictions caused by these evil practices is the Trinity (333) – God, The Father; Jesus Christ, The Son; and The Holy Spirit. I am a survivor of spiritual afflictions. Such experiences led to the formation of Works Of Trinity – a company fashioned by The Trinity, will be guided by The Trinity, and designed by The Trinity to take people through the last days when they are faced with increased spiritual warfare and the "*bitter cup of salvation*" (Reid---"God's Mission").

Advertisement for God's business will draw from an article in Astronomy.com that highlighted the discovery of a rare star-making galaxy that is producing stars at the rate of 4,000 per year. This is against the common Hierarchical Model theory of galaxy formation ("Rare star-making galaxy found").

God's business – Works Of Trinity, LLC, is one such rare star. One that, through the power of The Holy

Spirit will logistically locate those in need of deliverance and execute God's work.

I consider myself to be the first product of Works Of Trinity, LLC. However, I am not for sale. I am only on display for The Trinity. My experiences speak to this.

The idea of adding branded merchandise to the company's list of products came about after I viewed a blog of a co-worker who featured one of her clients who depended on our company for *"on time"* delivery of their products. Their products consisted of artifacts and special merchandise for their clients' events. To add to this, I saw a video of a new commercial in which there was the showing of logistical worldwide movement to achieve *"on time"* delivery of customers' products.

The key words, *"on time,"* resonated with me because I had discovered the nature of *"on time"* deliverance by The Trinity, from spiritual attacks. From knowing that the power of God has no barriers and extends throughout the world; having experiences of God putting things together in perfect order to achieve *"on time"* deliverance of individuals, such as me from situations; reading the article about the unusual birthing of 4,000 new stars per year by a planet; being directed by God to have a *"red"* star in the company's logo; knowing about the covering of the *"Blood of Jesus Christ"* which was shed on the cross; and being commissioned by Jesus Christ to write His books; I put it all together to define the representation of Works Of Trinity's logo.

The *"red"* stars in the logo for Works Of Trinity represent the *"Blood of Jesus Christ of Nazareth."* The logistical movements of the stars locate individuals, worldwide, for *"on time"* deliverance from spiritual, physical, natural, and social afflictions. Its movements will be initiated by the anointed and appointed spiritual soldiers in the Army of the Lord. As products of Works Of Trinity with its logo get delivered to individuals, they carry the prayers of God's company to provide Divine deliverance from the various issues individuals are facing.

It is not the first time God would be using a star to execute His work on earth. After Jesus Christ was born, God used a star to alert the wise men of His birth. Later, by logistical movement of the same star, God guided the wise men to the place where Jesus Christ was (Mathew 2: 9-10). As God used a Heavenly star to do the work of announcing an important event and to provide guidance in Biblical days, He is ready to use earthly stars to execute His works of *"on time"* deliverance for people.

God rules over all the earth. Likewise, as He enters commercial business He will rule over all businesses, throughout the world. God has chosen me to be owner and president of His business. However, He made it clear to me that all business activities of His company will be ONLY as authorized by Him. In the natural sense, I am not qualified to be conducting physical business since business was not the career path I chose. However, God qualified me for His spiritual business by choosing me to go on *"His mission"* and then using my experiences to establish His business – through book publishing and other activities He will be directing. I know that I will be passing on this business directly to Jesus Christ, as indicated in a dream I had in which I passed on a business bag which God gave me, to Jesus. The detail of this dream is in chapter 22.

*Chapter 10*

# God's Special Marketing Strategy

God knows of my limitations in business. Therefore, He did not leave it up to me to devise His marketing strategy for getting maximum sales and competitive advantage. Already God allowed me to be trained spiritually, now He turned His attention to my natural capabilities. He saw it fit to have me trained in the marketing strategy He selected for His business.

After choosing His marketing strategy, God made sure I attended a class. Although I know that God is God and can do anything, I am always amazed at the way He directs me. No company executive in the world can execute a plan of action as I have seen with God. The way He put together Divine connections for me to learn His marketing strategy is no exception. God's marketing strategy cannot be reproduced by any company executive.

Around April 11, 2011, I got an invitation in the mail to a seminar for presentation of *"Secrets of An Internet Millionaire"* by Anthony Morrison, to be held on Thursday, May 5, 2011 at the Holiday Inn, Hasbrouck Heights, New Jersey. I decided to call and reserve my seat since it mentioned the "New Wave" of social media advertising. I knew I would be using social media to advertise Works Of Trinity, since God had told me His business must be modern. However, I wasn't currently using any of them.

On April 18, 2011, I got a letter at my address from the seminar, but with my niece's name. I saw that the mail was confirmation of the seminar for which I signed up. I right away knew it was meant for me, but it was sent with the wrong name. I knew this was a spiritual incident God used to signal me to pay attention to this seminar. I have come to learn God has unpredictable ways of getting me to pay attention to certain things.

In less than an hour of seeing this mail, my same niece with the seminar name issue called me. She said that an application I had helped her to prepare more than a week ago was returned because she did not sign it. I told her to come to my house, so I could look at it. I found it hard to believe I missed having her sign the application and her husband who did the final review of the application also missed her signature problem. I immediately recognize this as a Divine connection – me getting confirmation for the seminar which was confused with her name and shortly after which she called me about a problem with her name. I took this as a serious re-enforcement of God's desire for me to pay special attention to the seminar.

I thought God had done enough to draw my attention to the *"Secrets of An Internet Millionaire"* seminar. However, He had more things planned. He knew my occasional habit and expectation to win the lottery. God used dreams to further emphasize the importance of the upcoming seminar to Him. On April 27, 2011, I had a dream of my sister, Catreen, telling me some of the lottery numbers; and previously, I had a dream in which I won the lottery and a dream with checks falling from the sky, in which my sister, Ruth, and I took them to the bank and then realized one million dollars was missing (Reid---"God Works Through Dreams"). Based on the more recent dream, I decided to play my numbers. I had gotten tired of playing and not wining, so I only play when there was some indication I might win.

On May 3, 2011, just as I pulled out the lottery ticket and turned on my computer to check the website for the winning numbers, the phone rang. I put it on speaker and heard a voice notification reminding me of the conference I registered for. The message indicated the speaker will teach me to be a millionaire. Once again, I see God making Divine connection; using my expectation of being a millionaire through winning the lottery to emphasize once again the importance of me going to the *"Secrets of An Internet Millionaire"* seminar. I realized, I will not necessarily win the lottery to become a millionaire, but will be taught how to become one.

On May 4, 2011, the day before the important *"Secrets of An Internet Millionaire"* seminar, I got a voice message from the same niece with the previous name connection to this seminar. She was asking me to deposit some checks for her the next day.

In the night I dreamt, *I was at an open space with many small rocks. There was a white building to my right. There were many oriental people outside, mostly women. They started jumping around. I knew they were filled with The Holy Spirit. One of the women came close to me. As she continued to move around in the Holy Spirit, her gray/purplish panty started falling. She would pull it up each time as she continued moving around in the Holy Spirit.*

The next day, May 5, 2011, after work I went to the bank and deposited four checks; each less than ten dollars. My niece had explained to me that she had overpaid on some of her bills and got refunded for the overpayments. I next went to the *"Secrets of a Millionaire"* seminar wearing the same outfit I wore at the dedication for Works Of Trinity to indicate to God that I got His message about the importance of this event to Him. I even brought His business checkbook because I knew these events usually ended up offering to sell something. I knew whatever it would be; God wanted me to have it.

I arrived too early for the event. When I went to the conference room, the host told me to wait outside until they were ready to start registering. I went and sat in front of the TV and watched the news on CNN. They were featuring President Obama's visit to the Fire Station in Manhattan, New York, because they had lost some members during the September 11 attacks.

About five minutes after I signed in, the fire alarm went off. People had to leave the building. I waited outside. While I was outside, the Bergen Fire Company came. Everybody had to gather outside in the parking lot. Later, a PSE&G utility vehicle showed up. After a while, I stayed in my car and read until they decided to call us back into the building. Later, I made a Divine connection with the spiritual fire incident and the dream I had about being on the outside of a place; seeing oriental people jumping around in The Holy Spirit; and seeing small rocks around. The rocks were the cars in the parking lot where people had to gather. God was notifying me of His presence at the event. I was not alone.

The seminar started about half an hour late due to the fire alarm activity. In the seminar, I saw three oriental people, which served to further confirm my dream involving oriental people, small rocks, and The Holy Spirit. We were introduced to affiliate marketing in which you advertise for companies on the internet and get small payments, most of the time.

When a real-time account was demonstrated, I saw that for many of the advertisements, you get paid less than ten dollars when the viewer took the required action. I immediately recalled that God allowed me to go to the bank to deposit checks in small amounts so that I would make the connection that this was what He wanted me to get involved in.

At the end of the seminar we were asked to sign up for a 3-day class in Piscataway, New Jersey. Based on the spiritual incidents with me getting confirmation for the event – with error involving my niece's name; getting a phone message from the sponsor of the event just as I decided to check on my lottery ticket and the sponsor speaking about being a millionaire; having my niece with the name connection asked me to deposit small amount of money on the day of the seminar which allowed me to grasp the idea of getting paid in small amount of money, as demonstrated in the seminar; and seeing the fire activity at the seminar just after I signed in; I decided God confirmed in many ways He wanted me to be involved in whatever business idea they would presented at the seminar.

Not surprising, 3-day workshop on affiliate marketing was introduced. The cost was $1995 for two people. In trying to find someone to split the cost, I met two Japanese men and one Japanese woman, which was further confirmation of the dream about the group of oriental people – a dream I had already connected to this seminar. Even though I failed in finding someone to split the cost, I did not hesitate to sign up for the 3-day workshop on affiliate marketing – the main reason for the seminar.

That night after the seminar, through a spiritual incident, Jesus Christ confirmed that He was the One directing me to proceed with the affiliate marketing venture. While sleeping, I became conscious of myself placing both my hands over my mouth and then cried out, "*Ohhh*," but not in a scared way. I was sleeping on my back at the time and with this action I also turned to my left. My daughter, Sonia, heard the sound and came to my bedside. She asked, "*What happened?*" I told her I knew somebody was coming towards me.

After a few minutes, I went back to sleep. Shortly after that, I woke up saying, "*In the name of Jesus Christ of Nazareth; in the name of Jesus Christ of Nazareth.*" After this, I went back to sleep within half an hour without further interruption. This was not the first time Jesus confirmed what action He wanted me to take by allowing my spirit to speak out in this way.

God continued to show me Divine connections to affiliate marketing while attending the 3-day class on this marketing strategy. On the second day of the seminar, we were introduced to a package with access to the software we would need to help us do business as affiliate marketers. I did not hesitate to buy it. However, since the package gave access to two people, an oriental woman approached me and was trying to persuade me to let her partner with me and share the cost of the package. She did not have enough money to buy it on her own. The coach advised her against it when we approached him to get his opinion.

This was a spiritual incident that links to the dream I had in which oriental people were dancing around in The Holy Spirit outside a building and one woman came very close to me as she continued to dance in The Holy Spirit. God used this spiritual incident to make yet another Divine connection to the importance of this affiliate marketing seminar; I knew He wanted me to attend.

On the third day of class, May 15, 2011, through spiritual incident, God emphasized the key area of the class to which He wanted me to pay attention. The teacher was on the topic of geographic targeting when I started feeling a desperate need to go to the bathroom. However, I did not want to miss what he was teaching. I made Divine connection to this area of training when the teacher said, "*I know I am taking a little longer than usually, but I just want to finish this topic before the break. Some of you might be waiting to go to the bathroom.*"

The Holy Spirit of God allowed me to make further Divine connection to the strategy of affiliate marketing in conducting His business when we were told of the affiliate network to which we would get automatic acceptance, after applying. The affiliate network, Wolf Storm, was named after an animal I dreamt about in 2005. This is written about in my book, *God Works Through Dreams*. In so many ways, God clearly demonstrated that affiliate marketing is His strategy to build His business. I know that once Works Of Trinity, LLC (God's business) is properly launched, He will be allowing me to make Divine connections with other businesses of His choosing. I expect that it would be of similar nature to the affiliate marketing class that God directed me to take.

*Chapter 11*

# Divine Connections

God's method of directing me in setting up His business is through Divine connections, using dreams and spiritual incidents. He may introduce other methods later, but for now, this is how He is training me to recognize when He is at work; so that I can increase in the knowledge of Him.

## Childhood to Womanhood

God's business consists of making Divine connections in an *"on time"* manner. He has been training me to recognize when He is making such connections to execute His business. I can relate numerous examples of God's *"on time"* spiritual incidents, which He uses to train me. People may want to call these *"coincidences."* However, when dreams and thoughts are constantly connected to wakening experiences in an *"on time"* manner, you know these events cannot be *"coincidences."* When you are well-connected to God your life is full of *"on time"* spiritual incidents.

In my first book, *God Works Through Dreams*, I wrote about the *"unforgettable dream"* I had when I was about four years old. *It was about Jesus Christ coming to me through the sun and then telling me something. I forgot what Jesus said to me. However, I never forgot the dream because of not just Who I dreamt about but because of the exhilarating feeling I got from His presence and what He said to me* (Reid--- "God Works Through Dreams"). When I gave the manuscript to be edited, the editor told me I should not just mention the dream like that. I should make a connection to my current life. Apparently, God spoke through her.

On August 26, 2010, I attended a convention at my church. There were visitors from other churches. A little girl who was about four years sang a song which included the words, *"He comes to me. Jesus comes to me."* I cried because I realized this was the connection for which my editor was asking. When I was a little girl, around the same age, Jesus had come to me. Through this little girl, Jesus allowed me to realize that what He told me as a little girl had manifested in the numerous spiritual battles I was undergoing in my adult life. This resulted in me going into business on behalf of God, due to such experiences. The little girl at the convention was wearing a red blouse and I was wearing a red T-shirt. I noticed God sometimes make connection with me and others by what they wear. Jesus did not only use this little girl to connect me to the dream I had of Him when I was around the same age, but He provided concrete confirmation of my thinking that the dream was connected to my experiences with spiritual battles.

Further confirmation of the childhood dream with adult manifestation took place on Sunday, April 8, 2012. I attended Easter Sunday service at the Presbyterian Church, which is featured in the dream I had as a little girl about Jesus coming to me through the sun. I was given time to do a mini-book presentation and I chose to mention this dream, which I had written about.

I was dressed according to how God directed me – in white and gold colors with my hair braided in the form of His Company's logo. After the service was over, a member of the congregation told me that he recognized the "*Star of David*" braided in my hair and later showed me the "*Prayer of David*" and its symbol, which has a circle around it. He explained to me that the circle around the "*Star of David*" was the sun. I immediately realized Jesus Christ was faithful to allow me to connect my youthful dream of Him coming out of the sun to the business I had established for God, because of my experiences with spiritual wickedness.

Although I am owner and president of God's business, my natural being does not know the full extent of His plans for me. In a dream, Jesus revealed the list of spiritual attributes He wants me to have. On October 28, 2010, I dreamt, *I saw my cousin, Liza. She showed me a list of things. I did not get to read them. She told me. "These are what Jesus wants me to have." I then found myself with a long list of things. I knew Jesus wants me to have them. I thought to myself, "I don't even know about these."*

Jesus has revealed to my spirit the spiritual gifts He has given to me. However, my mind is not aware of much of what I have been given. They get manifested in the spirit, as needed, to execute God's work. I know that the Holy Spirit of God works through me to do His work.

On the night following God's company's dedication, He allowed me to see His Holy Spirit as He enters me. That night, just before I fell asleep, I saw a golden band of light encircling my body. I then felt an enlightening feeling as it entered my body. The feeling lasted a few minutes. I then fell asleep, peacefully.

The sensation of The Holy Spirit reminded me of when I was with a psychologist. I was telling her of how I had to call on the name of Jesus when faced with evil spirits. In that moment, an enlightening feeling rose from deep within my chest and rested on my face. The psychologist commented that my face lit up when I spoke of Jesus (Reid---"God's Mission"). As I move forward in conducting God's business, His Spirit will arise from within me to do the work.

My level of spirituality in God was not attained through the teachings of humans. I did not have to memorize catechisms, symbols, or rituals. The Spirit of God (Holy Spirit) that dwells within me executes all the works, through me. The Holy Spirit provides direction as to what needs to be done and takes control of me, in an *"on time"* manner. When the Holy Spirit arises within me and speaks, or makes spiritual movements, the actions are directly related to accomplishing the works of God. I don't even have to know what I am being led to do. However, God usually gives me a hint.

## Healing

Through Divine connections, God showed me how He will heal those He points out to me to pray for. On January 4, 2011, while I was at work, Janet, a co-worker, who is a Christian, came to me during lunch and said she was asking me to pray for her friend, Jasmine, who was in the hospital. Janet was afraid Jasmine might die. She was on a respirator due to a cold she did not take care of early enough, which turned into viral infection and breathing complications. She was also diabetic.

After Janet left, I remembered the dream I had about Joe with his sick family member whom I was supposed to heal. On January 1, 2011, I dreamt, *I was in a room. Joe, a Jewish co-worker, was also in the room. I looked to my left and saw an image of a small white boy, about four years old. I knew he was related to Joe. I found myself with a black bag, typical of what doctors usually carry. I knew I had to go and heal the little boy. I started to walk away with the bag.*

Since Joe sat in the same aisle as Janet, I wondered if this dream was meant for her. After Janet came back from lunch, I stopped by her desk and told her the dream. I told her I thought the dream was meant for her and that her friend would get better because I prayed for her.

Not long after I returned to my desk, Joe came to see his manager who sat across from me. I overheard pieces of the conversation, which indicated that he had a family member who was sick and in the hospital.

*Divine Connections*

Later, I stopped by Joe's desk and told him of the dream I had about him and a sick family member. He told me his mother-in-law had a heart attack on January 1, 2011 and he only got a call about it today. I asked him for his mother-in-law's name, so I could pray for her. He gave it to me.

I ended up praying for healing, in the name of Jesus, for both Joe's mother-in-law and Jasmine. As it turned out, it was not long after that Jasmine died. However, Joe's mother-in-law recovered from her heart attack. God used these spiritual incidents to demonstrate to me He would heal those He points out to me to pray for and not necessarily those for whom I decide to pray.

Later I got confirmation from God as to why He wanted me to pray for someone who is Jewish. On January 14, 2011, I went to Matt Sorger's conference in Long Island, New York. David Herzog was the guest speaker. He said that we should start praying for the Jews as that would cause God to respond more to our prayers. I made Divine connection with what he said to the dream I had about Joe, which led me to pray for his Jewish mother-in-law who recovered from her illness. On the other hand, Jasmine who I also prayed for did not recovery from her illness.

## Business Meeting

One aspect of doing business is to have meetings. With God's business, it is no different. On July 25, 2011, I was running late for bed because I had my hair braided. It was finished a few minutes after 10:00 p.m. I decided that although it was late, and I did not get much sleep the previous night, I would stay up to complete the writing I started about *"Holy Spirit Fire"* – a chapter in this book. However, I decided it would be best if I took a shower first.

While taking my shower, I was thinking that the next day was payday, so I would have the money to make my contribution to my church's bills, which were outstanding. I thought of calling my bishop the next day to ask him if he could come and pick up the check from me, or if he could wait until the coming Friday. If he could wait until Friday, I would just decide to go to Prophet Inka's meeting in the neighborhood, although I didn't really feel like going. I had a lot of work to do. While showering and thinking I was singing in my mind, *"Alleluia, alleluia, worthy is the lamb, worthy is the lamb, amen."*

After finishing my shower, I found myself repeating, *"Alleluia Lord Alleluia."* As I added lotion to my hands, I continued to repeat those words. After a while, my left hand held on to my right hand. My left hand formed a circle around the fingers of my right hand, with all touching each other. I stayed like this for a very long time while repeating, "*Alleluia Lord Alleluia.*" After a while, I found myself saying, "*Thank you Lord*" for quite a while.

Next, I found myself bowing my head with my hands still holding onto each other. After a while, I found myself saying, "*Yes Jesus,*" a few times. I stayed with my head bowed for quite a while. Next, I found myself getting lowered. I positioned my body on the floor with my left leg raised and my right knee on the floor. My left hand rested on my left leg with its palm up and my right hand rested on my left hand. My head rested on my right hand.

I realized I was bowing down to God as He commune with my spirit. My spirit did not reveal what was taking place. I stayed in that anointed position for quite a while. All this time I was naked. It was not the first time that God has communed with me while I was naked. The first time was when I was in the shower, during an anointing (Reid---"God's Mission"). This time it was immediately after taking a shower.

The next day, while making notes on a sheet of paper about the incident after my shower the night before, it came into my spirit to put the title of "*Works Of Trinity Meeting*" on the paper. This was an indication God called a meeting with me, Jesus, and the Holy Spirit, just like directors would call meeting to discuss the affairs of their businesses. However, in God's meeting, it did not matter if I was naked or not. I am sure my spirit took note of what was said in the meeting. However, my physical mind had no idea of what was being communicated.

## Chapter 12
# My Job Preview

God allowed me to have a preview of what it would be like working fulltime for Him. I made this Divine connection through a dream and spiritual incidents at my current fulltime job. On May 30, 2011, I had a very brief dream in which, *I was at my mother's house. I was kneeling on the floor in the room adjoining my mother's room. I was feeling slightly achy and tired as I laid out a piece of cloth on the floor. My sister, Ruth, came in the room and said to me, "We are working this hard to prepare for next year."*

On June 10, 2011, I remembered this dream when I was feeling the same way at work. I was working on a project that was large in scope and we were short on time to complete it. Other team members had to be assigned to help me with it. I had to take time to train the two co-workers as to what they need to do to continue with what I started. I had to be working overtime to try to catch up with the work, but that was not enough.

## My Job Preview

Throughout the day, I was bombarded with my manager's Instant Message for progress; Dan coming to me with questions; being on status call with other groups while processing results for them; and my supervisor stopping by my desk to talk while I was on the status call working with the other group members. This was when I experienced the same feeling of tiredness while working, as in the dream.

God had shown me I would be very busy while working fulltime for Him. By spiritual incidents, He confirmed what is contained in my job description. On February 12, 2011, I went to my niece Berta's Saga Benefits dinner at her school. She belonged to a group that sponsors girls in Africa to go to school. One of the girls in the group went to Africa to visit with the girl whom the group was sponsoring.

At the benefit dinner, the girl reported on her visit to Africa. One thing she mentioned that really stood out was that the African girl's mother got sick with breast infection. The bush doctor told her she would have to literally bring the hand of one of her family members for her mother to get better. The African girl could not do it and her mother died.

The African girl told the girl from the U.S.A. to promise her there would be no bush doctors in her country.

The U.S.A. girl gave the African girl that promise. Bush doctor in Africa is like someone who works by devious spiritual means, such as witchcraft, or voodoo.

I started to think that the promise the U.S.A. girl gave the African girl could be the promise I made to God when I told Him I would help others who were going through the same experiences I had with spiritual wickedness. I asked myself, *"Does this translate to making sure there are no witchcraft or voodoo workers in the U.S.A.?"*

On our way home from the benefits dinner, it was dark. I had my niece, Lisa, in the front passenger seat to help me watch for the exits. When I was about to take exit 67 – Route 1/New Brunswick/ Trenton, my daughter, Sonia, who was in the back seat said to me, *"You don't want to take the exit to Trenton."* I got confused and thought I would be going south when I wanted to go north. I decided against taking the exit.

After driving some distance, I realized that was really the correct exit. It had both north and south. The problem was that it specified the names of two towns, which didn't tell much if you do not know which town was north and which was south. I came off the next exit and turned around.

We had another mishap with the next exit. After Lisa saw the exit sign for the Turnpike, she told me it was the next exit. I came off the exit and immediately realized this was not the correct one. I came off too early. I had to turn around once again. While driving along the Turnpike, I saw my fuel gauge was showing less than a quarter tank full. However, I figure it would last until I reached home.

After, I took the exit for my home; the yellow warning light for gas came on. Since I had to drop my sister, Petra, and her daughter, Lisa, home, I told Sonia I would just drop her off on the road where she could just cross over to our house, since the gas was low, and I wanted to get gas. She said she preferred to be dropped home, since it wasn't too far from home.

I decided to drop Sonia home. As I turned the corner at the light, we came across a tow truck parked on the right side of the road. A van was in front of it. Lisa read and spoke out that it was AAA. I glance to my right and saw that the AAA attendant had a red gas container in his hand. Obviously, the driver of the van had to call AAA because he or she ran out of gas.

Sonia said, *"This is creepy. We are about to run out of gas and now we see this."* To me, this was not creepy. I knew God had used this spiritual incident to make Divine connect with the thought I had at the benefit dinner. He wanted me to make sure there would be no bush doctors (Obeah men/women, witchcraft worker, voodoo priest, or any such workers of spiritual wickedness) in the U.S.A. At that time, I got the message, but God did not show or tell me how it would be accomplished.

About two years after the African bush doctors' connection, God gave me some idea of how He will be dealing with those who practice spiritual wickedness. I have had many experiences of suffering caused by those who practice spiritual wickedness. Satan is using them to destroy others and themselves. When they practice the art of spiritual wickedness, they are serving Satan, not God. They do not know that Satan leads them astray from God because he wants them to go to Hell. Satan and his angels have already been sentenced to Hell (2 Peter 2:4; Revelation 20:1-3) and he is trying to drag us into sin so that we will also go there. On the other hand, Jesus came and died to redeem us from sin. He then went back to Heaven to prepare a place for us to be with Him, in Heaven (Titus 2:14; John 14:2-3).

The truth is that I was expecting God to rid this world of those who practice spiritual wickedness by allowing them to die. However, God has shown me that to do this would be to support Satan's work of destroying them. God has a plan of redemption for the spiritually wicked, just like everyone else. The Trinity (God, Jesus Christ, and the Holy Spirit) is in the business of reversing the works of Satan. This was shown to me with the same *"alleluia"* hymn (numbers 221 & 122) being reversed in the Chalice Hymnal and my old Presbyterian Hymnal (Reid---"God's Mission").

God has shown me that He will be using me to reverse the works of Satan with the spiritually wicked by ministering to them about the Trinity. As they turn aside from Satan and serve God, there will be no more spiritually wicked workers in the U.S.A., as promised to God. He gave me the opportunity to experience ministering to the spiritually wicked and then confirmed that He will arrest them in their activities by allowing me to hear of the arrest of such a person, in an *"on time"* manner. Here is the story.

In January 2014, one of my relatives was experiencing constant spiritual attacks. At first, my sister, Ruth, was talking to him and praying with him. She suggested that I call him and tell him of what I had been through with spiritual attacks. I called and told him about some of the experiences, which I had been through. Next,

Ruth suggested that we pray together for our relative for three consecutive days.

On the first night of praying, I asked God to allow me to help others as I had promised Him to do. That night, God showed me what to do to help my relative and his family. Starting that night, God would wake me up at nights to defend my relative when he was under attack; using spiritual movements with my hands. My relative was able to sleep at nights while I dealt with what came against him. Because of this, a demon visited me on January 31, 2014, trying to negotiate with me. I woke up around 4:00 a.m. in the morning as I became aware of a spirit that was not hostile.

I was lying on my back. I stretched out my left hand in a fist and said, "*So, you know who I am. So, you have never seen anyone like me before.*" That was the start of a very long conversation between the spirit and me. During the conversation, I would hear myself speak and repeat back what the spirit said. It was a spirit-to-spirit conversation because my mind didn't know what the spirit was saying to me. I only knew of what I spoke out in response to the spirit. It was as if the spirit was questioning who I was.

I started speaking while lying on my back then rose up to a sitting position as I continue to speak to the spirit. My legs were apart, and knees slightly bent. I sometimes made circles with both hands between my legs and with all my fingers outstretched.

I told the spirit, *"I take instructions direct from Heaven. Stop all evil activities. Satan knows me. Satan challenged God to take over from Him; so, God cast him out of Heaven with the angels who agreed with him. God created Heaven and earth. He is in charge of the music industry; education and others."* The spirit was acting as if it did not know about God. I said, *"Jesus came and died to redeem people from sins. He will be coming back as Adonai. He spoke the words to create everything on earth. Words will obey Him."* I told the spirit that, *"Words will not be used for evil anymore. Words will only be used for good."* I repeated several times with emphasis while doing circular motion with my hands and rocking. As if chanting, I said, *"All of God's creation will obey Him. They will not be used for evil anymore. Creation will turn against those who are using them for evil."* I told the spirit, *"Read the Bible. Read the Bible. Those who opposed Moses when he was doing God's work were swallowed up by the ground."*

I repeatedly asked the spirit, *"Why did you mess with this family?"* I said, *"Confess to God. He knows all that you have done but you have to confess to Him. Speak it to Him. God will forgive, but you have to confess to Him."*

It was as if the spirit was trying to negotiate with me. I heard myself spoke out strongly, *"No negotiation, no negotiation, no negotiation; direct from Heaven, nothing else; direct from Heaven, nothing else. God sent me to deal with all the evil spirits to get rid of them. I am a killer of demons and I could kill you right now. God sent me to get rid of people who are doing spiritual wickedness against others. Spread the word so that others will know that they will be destroyed it they do not turn away from their evil ways."* I had my fingers locked together in a triangle as I spoke this and pushed it forward while speaking.

I told the spirit, *"Confess and ask for forgiveness. There is forgiveness if you ask God to forgive you. Turn away from your evil ways. Turn to God and confess. There will be consequences if you don't give up your wicked ways. There is no escape; even your very self will go against you."* I emphasized and repeated to the spirit that, *"Any decision you make will go against you. Run and hide. Run and hide. Run and hide."*

I told the spirit, *"Speak your name. Who are you? Who are you? Speak your name. Speak your name."* I started to get impatient as the spirit refused to respond. I said, *"It must be that God is allowing me to testify to you."* I was sensing that I was speaking to the spirit that was doing harm against my relative, spiritually. I was speaking for so long and pressing it to identify itself, but I was running out of patience. I told the spirit, *"I am not going to linger much longer with you."* Again, I asked the spirit to tell me its name. However, it did not respond. I started to count 1, 2, 3, 4, 5, 6. I stopped at 6 and repeated, *"666, 666; we have met before. Run and hide. Run and hide."* I ended the conversation as I realized it was the 666 demon.

Later in the morning, I turned on the radio in my car on my way to work. I heard on 1010 WINS that police arrested a psychic from Ridgewood, New Jersey, who cheated her client out of $150, 000 by telling the client, she would get rid of demons out of her. I knew God was faithful in allowing me to hear this to confirm what I had said to the 666 demon. In effect, God will be arresting the spiritually wicked; allowing them to turn from Satan and accept Jesus as their redeemer; or, suffer the consequence of their wicked ways.

Later in the day, I heard from Ruth that our relative was attacked in the night. The 666 demon had kept me engaged in conversation so I would not defend my relative while another demon attacked him. This was a wicked spiritual strategy. However, no spiritual strategy can outdo that of the Trinity – The Head of all principality and power (Colossians 2:10). After this encounter with an evil spirit and me ministering to it, God led me to the stories of Elaine and Rebecca in the book, *He Came to Set The Captives Free*, by Rebecca Brown, MD.

In this book, as a baby, Elaine's mother sold her blood to a satanic cult, unknowingly. This led to Elaine being possessed by demons and her later involvement with the occult. She rose quickly to become the top bride of Satan within the U.S.A. She did spiritual wickedness to other people, such as Rebecca Brown, MD, the other main character in the book. The part of Elaine's story that stood out to me the most is when she astral projected her spirit body and joined with other witches *"to kill a family who was converting cult members to Jesus Christ."* Elaine saw *"the family's defense of powerful linked angels, which she and the other participating witches could not get pass. One angel spoke to her to accept Jesus as her Lord and warned her that if she continued with what she was doing she would be destroyed because Satan hates her, but Jesus loves her"* (Brown 57).

God is extremely faithful in correcting me in my wrong thinking. After He allowed me to witness to an evil spirit, He led me to the book which showed me that Jesus Christ also came to save the spiritually wicked. Like Rebecca Brown in the book, God is going to use me to reverse the works of Satan by witnessing to the spiritually wicked and converting them to Jesus Christ. This way Satan's kingdom on earth would be destroyed by disarming his key people (Obeah men/women, witchcraft workers, voodoo priests, false prophets, or any such workers of spiritual wickedness) he uses to carry out his works. Spiritually wicked people carry out spiritual wickedness, using evil spirits, including demons, and their spirit-self (Brown).

God has unlimited ways of allowing me to pay special attention to something – through dreams, thoughts, spoken words, people, or situation. He makes Divide connections, using spiritual incidents. God has dominion over everything. He has shown me to use *"stars"* in His company's logo to indicate His movements around the world to accomplish His works.

## My Job Preview

On April 28, 2011, during a special presentation at my current job, God allowed me to receive messages in my spirit as having a preemptive claim to logistics, making decisions involving the *"unknown,"* not having any fear of the unknown, having a team of Heavenly host to watch my back, having unknown partners generating creative solution, and embracing *"social media"* as a vehicle for promoting His business. In effect, God was telling me He had all logistics planned for His business. I did not have to be afraid of any unknown because I would be working with a Heavenly team – I would not be doing His works alone. God has creative solutions for His business and I should use *"social media"* to advertise His business.

*Chapter 13*
# The House of God

If you have not realized this yet, I would like to point out to you that everything on this earth belongs to God; including yourself and what you seemingly work very hard to possess. You might be familiar with the concept of *"eminent domain"* when it comes to the government repossessing your property, for a valid reason. It is hardly likely that anyone would be happy with such actions. It is better for us to think of ourselves as keepers of what we have. At any time, God can take what is His and give to another, or do whatever, He pleases with it.

I found out that sometimes you might not want something for yourself, but God wants you to have it. After I separated from my husband, I was trying to get him to take over the house. However, he couldn't afford to do so. I then tried persuading him to sell it, but the housing market was very bad, and we could not even sell it for the current mortgage balance. We negotiated a settlement agreement before our divorce and I ended up with the house, since I was at least able to pay the mortgage on my own. However, I had no intention of keeping it. I got a *"For Sale by Owner"* sign and decided I would try to sell it myself. I was hoping someone would be willing to buy it at the current mortgage amount.

As it turned out, I did not even get the chance to put up my *"For Sale by Owner"* sign. I was too busy at work to be showing people the house, so I kept putting it off. In the meantime, God was directing me to do things with the house.

God directed me with spiritual incidents and dream to paint the doors of my house *"red."* I now call it, *"The House of God."* On October 18, 2010, I was telling Ruth I was thinking of painting the doors of my house in *"red"* because God had been constantly allowing me to acquire *"red"* things. Ruth suggested I do the garage door but not the house doors. However, I knew in my spirit that God wanted me to paint my house doors in *"red."* I was also told by a church member the Holy Spirit revealed to her that *"red"* was my color. Furthermore, in the evening I had experienced a spiritual incident with a co-worker with whom I carpooled. There was a lot of traffic on our way home. He decided to try and find a back road to make it home because after going home he would have to take his family somewhere far.

He took the next exit, which had the divider in the middle paved *"red."* My co-worker made several turns to try to find a shortcut. He ended up at a house with the door painted in *"red."* I made Divine connections with the very first time getting into such heavy traffic since we started carpooling; turning off on a road with *"red"* divider; and then be drawn to a house with the door painted *"red."* We ended up going back to the highway with the lot of traffic because that exit just went into some twists and turns and led back to the highway.

After leading us to a house with the door painted *"red,"* that night, God re-emphasized with a dream, His desire for me was to paint the doors of His house *"red."* I dreamt, *I was thinking about the spiritual incident in my church the past Sunday in which I took part in casting out demons from a woman who came to ask for prayer. I thought we should have a "red" bucket with water to direct the demons into it and prevent them from entering other people. I started speaking, "In the name of Jesus," about three times.*

At that point, I woke up and removed the cover from my face. As I did this, I saw my daughter, Sonia, standing just at the doorway of my room, wrapped in a *"red"* blanket. Although she was concerned about my outburst and did not understand the significance of what happened, I knew immediately this was a well-timed spiritual incident in which God was clearly showing me to have the doors painted in *"red."* He allowed Sonia to stand at the door, covered in *"red,"* at the time I was calling on Jesus. I know Jesus usually lets me speak out His name when He wants to give me confirmation that He is the One Who is making the request of me.

Soon after this, I acted on God's desire to have the doors of His house painted in *"red."* I was commanded to do so in the name of Jesus. I made the Divine connection that the *"red"* color represented the blood of Jesus and offers Divine protection.

Soon after the painting project, God clearly indicated to me He wanted me to start a business at my house. He then directed me to the publishing method I should use by sending a messenger with a book to steer me to His chosen path for His business. After the realization that God wanted me to be a book publisher, I immediately started setting up the basement to be used as His office. I started on January 8, 2011.

It did not take long for God to let me know in no uncertain term that this was His *"other house."* I made this Divine connection through a dream. On January 11, 2011, I dreamt, *I was in a car with a young black woman. She was giving me a ride home from church. She stopped near my house.*

*As I was about to get out of the car I said to her, "I won't be going back to church because I have a lot to do." I knew she would be going to the evening service. I knew she lived near me and had two houses. I said to her, "Show me your other house."*

*We both got out of the car and walked a short distance. She showed me a small multi-story structure that consisted of metal framing. The lowest level of the structure had a red wooden door. I said to her, "They are working on it." she replied, "Only one piece is put in." She walked away in anger, leaving me in front of the house structure, staring at it.*

I knew this dream meant I should not be concerned about missing church on Sundays to get the work done on God's other house – my basement. The entrance door to my basement was painted in red and at the time of the dream only mental frames were up.

This dream made Divine connection to a dream my cousin, Liza, had about me. She called to tell me the dream at the end of the same day I started work on God's house. In her dream, *I called her and told her to tell her son, Tom, to hurry up because they were waiting on him.* I connected the *"hurry up"* request in Liza's dream to the dream I had of the woman who looked at a house being built and was angry that not enough progress was made. Also, I connected Tom in Liza's dream to one of the men who was helping me to setup the basement. Like Tom, he also had 3-month old baby. This allowed me to realize God wanted me to hurry up with setting up the basement – His office. God was in a hurry to have His other house, but I didn't know why. I did what I could to pitch in and get the work done faster.

I had the dedication for Works Of Trinity, LLC on March 19, 2011. I invited my family and the men who setup God's office. My sister, Ruth, helped me put the event together. She bought a bouquet of flowers and placed it at one of the windows. One of the guests who attended the dedication had to come directly from a wedding he had attended earlier in the day. Two important events happened after the dedication; my nephew showed me a picture of Jesus as a Black man; later, just before going to sleep, God allowed me to see His Holy Spirit as a golden band of light before He entered my body.

After the dedication, I started buying fresh flowers at the farmer's market weekly and put them at three windows. Soon, for the first time in fourteen years, my lawn started growing a lot of wild flowers which were yellow and white. I realized God wanted to emphasize He wanted flowers in His house. One day while at a wholesale store, my eyes were drawn to orchid flowers in pots. I decided to buy three of them and put at the windows of God's house. This way, all I had to do was to remember to give them a little water.

After I placed the orchid flowers in God's house, I had to cut the lawn. When the grass started growing again I noticed only very few of the wild flowers survived. With the next cut of the lawn, all wild flowers disappeared. God had certainly pointed out to me in dreams and with spiritual incidents that He wanted flowers in His house. He had seriously taken possession of the office I dedicated as His place of business. Whenever, I entered God's office I would get an elated feeling of Holiness – God was occupying His house.

After I completed setting up God's office, He led me to a special teaching by Matt Sorger. My daughter,

Kristal, had asked me to take her to Matt Sorger's conference in Long Island, New York, on January 13, 2012. I did not remember what time the conference would start so I decided to search the internet for *"Matt Sorger"* to get information on this conference. I came across Matt's April 2006 Teachings and decided to read it.

In his teachings, Matt mentioned God speaking through prophets such as Haggai and Joshua, the high priest, to build His temple so that He could be glorified. Matt wrote of the desire *"to build a house in which God's glory can dwell" on earth...God's people arising "to offer their lives in a new and deeper way as a living habitation for God's presence and glory. People will even be willing to make sacrifice so that God's glory can have a dwelling place in the earth, through their lives"* (Sorger--- "Awakening"). I knew I had made tremendous sacrifices in establishing God's business, so received this message.

Matt then warned us not to compare what God does now to show His glory, or how He does it in our time with what He did in Biblical time (Haggai 2:3; 2 Chronicles 5:14). In that, we should not be looking to see something like Solomon's temple. Matt further warned us not to compare past moves of God with current moves of God so that we can see His greater glory in the way He chooses to display it. Matt encouraged us to be sensitive to movements of the Holy Spirit so that we wouldn't miss them. After all, the glory of God's later temple would be greater than the one before (Sorger---"Awakening").

By Divine spiritual incident, God led me to Matt's April 2006 Teachings, so I could relate Matt's prophesies to what I had done for God. God likes to challenge us. We were challenged to believe that Jesus was the Messiah when He was born in a stable, to a poor family. Let us now embrace the challenge of God establishing His business on earth in a basement – taking on the *"Home Business"* concept compared to a *"Fortune 500 Business"* concept. When I started setting up His office, God was quick in telling me, in a dream, it was His other house. God has effectively exercised *"eminent domain"* over my house. It truly belongs to Him, as I kept and prepared it just for Him.

Before finalizing this book file, God was faithful to lead me to a Biblical example of the meaning of this chapter's title, which I did not realized was chosen by Him. I thought I came up with the title, based on knowing that I kept the house because I realized God wanted to. However, He allowed me to learn that I was mistaken. I listened to the August 2014 monthly CD I got from Matt Sorger, which is entitled, *The Finished Work*. Matt's sermon was about Jacob's dream of, *a ladder from earth, extending to Heaven; angels were ascending and descending the ladder while God stood at the top of it and spoke to Jacob. God reassured Jacob that He would be with him always until what He spoke of is accomplished.*

After Jacob awoke, he realized that God was at that place, but he did not know it. He realized that the place was *"The House of God"* and *"The Gate of Heaven."* Jacob therefore called the place Bethel and made a vow to God (Sorger---"The Finished Work"). The scripture was from Genesis 28: 11-22.

My God is so powerful that after I wrote the sentence about Jacob making a vow to Him, He allowed by daughter who was suffering from a cold to come to my room and spoke to me. After she left, I felt that I was catching a cold and went to the kitchen to get orange juice and vitamin C. While in the kitchen, the Spirit of God came upon me. I rebuked the cold and then surrendered the house to God while making prophetic moves. Often when I struggled with taking care of the house, I would tell God that it was His house and I kept it for Him. With what just happened to me in the kitchen, I realized that God officially took control of His house, making it a gateway to Heaven.

*Chapter 14*
# A Special Editor

God has been giving me direction in putting together every aspect of His business. The book editing process is no exception. When I decided I would hire someone professional to edit the manuscript for my book, *God's Mission: Spiritual Battles and Revelation of Anti-666*, I did some research on the internet and then contacted a few potential editors. I sent a few pages as sample and asked them to use it to demonstrate the quality of their works.

I was satisfied with one editor's work, but she was not able to start as early as I would like. However, her price for editing was reasonable. One of the potential editors to whom I sent my sample was from a company I heard of before. I was pleased to discover they were located on the way to my current job. I waited a few days to hear from that company.

One day I decided to call my contact at the book editing company to hear the result of the evaluation of my manuscript. When I made the call and identified myself, he said he could not belief what just happened. He called it a word, which I do not remember. He explained that the moment he just finished evaluating my manuscript was the moment I called him. I knew there and then that this *"on time"* call was God's way of signaling me to use this company for the book editing. Knowing this, I did not hesitate to accept that company as the editor for my book. God had chosen it.

After making the Divine connection, I stopped by the book editing company on my way from work and signed the contract on January 30, 2011, for them to start working on my manuscript. I was assigned to a local editing manager, named James. I explained to him that the book was about my experiences with God and it was of Biblical equivalence. He told me that the Bible is one of a kind.

When I reached home, I saw a postcard from a company, BookMasters, which indicated that they print and publish books. I had already selected a printing company but decided to research this one on the internet. I was interested in what I read about them and decided to send an email to get further information. Interestingly, I was checking on their featured authors when I came across one

*A Special Editor*

who wrote about experiences he had with the Trinity. I could relate to some of the experiences he wrote about. However, I got the impression that he did not use an editor.

By spiritual incidents, God made Divine connection with me and this author to show His appreciation of me considering His works worthy of the best possible presentation by making the sacrifice of hiring an editor. I did not settle for the cheapest priced editor, but for the one God confirmed I should use. To accomplish this, I had to sell a little more than a third of the stocks I was trying to keep, in difficult economic times.

After this encouraging connection with the author, I took a break and did some house chores before going back to the internet to do further research on BookMasters. This time, I decided to pay attention to the search list that showed up when I typed the search word. In the search list, I saw a topic, "*Reid v. BookMasters.*" That really caught my attention because I have the same last name. I decided to click on it to get further information.

There was not much information about the case, so I decided to write the company to get an explanation of it. I mentioned that I was keeping an open mind about the case; I was going into business for the Trinity and as Directors, they would help me sort out any issues before I create partners. I knew God is not afraid of doing business with companies having issues since He knows how to straighten things out.

The president of the company wrote back and explained that the judge dismissed the case because the contract with the publisher was clear. She thought it was the company's job to sell her books. I was satisfied with his explanation because in my research about book publishing, it was clear to me I would have to be marketing my books. I considered this company to be a likely candidate with whom I could do business. However, I was not quite sure of this as I was with the editing company.

At that time, I did not know that God was only using the "*Reid v. BookMasters*" case to prepare me for an issue with the book editing company I had just contracted with. The managing editor assigned to my manuscript passed it on to an editor. The editor read it through and then called me to introduce himself. He interviewed me to get a better feel for the story. He mentioned that I should not use the abbreviation, "*WOT*," for Works Of Trinity since it would diminish what I am emphasizing to others. I immediately realized that what he said was true. God had only given me the abbreviation in a dream, so I could figure out the company's name when the time came for such a decision. I want to emphasize the *"works"* of the Trinity, consisting of Holy Spirit fire burning throughout the world, bringing souls to the true and living God. To do this, the entire name must be intact.

Later in my editing process, I made a Divine connection with the case of BookMasters and the contract issue they had with someone named, Reid. God allowed me to first sign my contract with the editing company and then show me later, by real-life example, that I would have an issue with my contract. However, when my issue arose I knew God was in control. I realized God wanted the editing manager of the company I had my book-editing contract with to be exposed to what I was writing.

When the editing process was almost half-way through, the editing manager left the company, giving only two weeks' notice. This caused some delays and uncertainty of the last edited manuscript. The editing manager was finally called to be a state trooper in Pennsylvania, which was his life-long dream. I had a good rapport with him and missed that. However, I saw that the plan of God was to expose law enforcement personnel to the sufferings of victims of spiritual wickedness, which is sadly outside of law enforcement's capabilities. Wicked people use devilish, spiritual means to injury, or even kill others without being punished by the law. Such people are really criminals who get away with crimes, which can be very serious. I know that later when I am conducting God's business; this former editing manager will come into play. He has gained the background knowledge he will need later in his work.

## Chapter 15
# Holy Spirit Fire

Many times, God uses multiple Divine connections to put a story together. I was able to link multiple dreams and multiple spiritual incidents to tell the story of Holy Spirit [Ghost] fire that will be sweeping throughout the U.S.A. and extend to the entire world.

The beginning of The Holy Spirit fire story is a dream I had on November 17, 2007, which I entitled, *"God Is Dancing"* and wrote in my book, *God Works Through Dreams*. The short version of this dream is that, *there was constant outbreak of small fires all around. After my daughter prayed, God came down from the sky in the form of a cartoon figure and began to dance for quite a while. It then began to rain, and the fires were quenched.* I saw the fulfillment of this dream in several satanic attacks, which I conquered and then began to dance in the Holy Spirit, declaring that I am a child of God.

The next Divine connection to this story is a dream I had on January 2, 2011 in which, *on the screen of my cell* phone, I saw a triangular flag, splattered with blood. I realized that the cell phone was about to explode so I threw it into an old tank at my mother's house. Immediately, there was a huge fire in the tank, but it was contained.

On the day following this huge fire in the tank dream, I bought a Gospel CD from a guest singer at my church. The next day I played it and heard a song that was all about fire. It calls on *"sons of God...children of God"* to arise from the ends of the earth with *"fire in your hands...fire in your mouth... fire in your feet...keep the fire burning by the power of God...everybody moving and grooving by the power of God...fire to the enemy"* (Lewis).

A few days later, I decided to rip this CD to my netbook computer and it showed up in Windows Media Player as *"Unknown album."* I then rename this album with the artist's name. His last name is Lewis. However, after doing the rename his name became added to Barbara Lewis' album icon and both names show for the album. The titles of the songs became those of Barbara Lewis'. I was very puzzled as to how this happened. I clicked on the number four song, now entitled *"Make Me Belong to You"* since for Lester Lewis it was the *"Fire"* song. I played that song and it turned out to be Lester Lewis' *"Fire"* song.

I thought it was interesting that the *"Fire"* song's title became superimposed with *"Make Me Belong to You."* I wrote in my book, *"Jesus, make me belong to you – fire."* I later looked up the lyrics of the Barbara Lewis' song. From it, I recognize the message that Jesus has the power to make me whatever He wants me to be. I can even be His puppet. I made Divine connection to this spiritual incident that I will be one of those who Jesus will be using as a *"Fire"* burning by the power of God and having everybody moving and grooving, by the power of God.

The next Divine connection to the *"Holy Spirit Fire"* story is in yet another dream in which it was clear that the *"Holy Spirit Fire"* will be operating in high places. Leaders in high positions will have to acknowledge that God exists.

In this dream, *I was high up in a multi-story building in a wide-open area. Suddenly, I noticed large flames of fire in front of me, coming from below the floor. I looked to my right and saw a red, circular fire alarm button on the wall. It was about six inches in diameter. I went and pressed hard on the fire alarm button and then turned back in the direction from which I came, to see if I could get out that way.*

*There were also large flames of fire beneath the floor in that direction. I was trapped in a corner with a huge fire in front and below me. The corner had roughly 8' x 10' of safety zone, which was without fire. There were windows on either side of the corner where I was standing. I was not feeling afraid even though the fire was raging around me.*

*Suddenly two white men were in the fire-free zone with me. After a while, it came to my thought to open a window. I opened it to let air in as the fire continued to burn. One of the white men said, "Now I know that God is real."*

The above dream indicating recognition of God in high places is supported by the Divine connection I made with Rick Joyner's prophetic dream and the shooting of Congresswoman Griffords. On January 7, 2011, I asked my daughter, Kristal, if she heard about the shooting of the congresswoman in Arizona. She commented that she was not surprised because she saw on Sid Roth's ministry a man who prophesied that things were going to happen to America (U.S.A.) in 2011. She showed me the video of an interview with Rick Joyner on Sid Roth's website.

Rick Joyner was explaining a vision he had about America, which worried him. His vision reminded me of my dreams of small fires popping up all over the place and God coming down in the form of a cartoon to quench it with rain; of huge fire in an old tank; and of a large blazing fire in a high-rise building, in which I was sounding the fire alarm.

In Rick's vision, *he was in a log cabin with each room representing a part of America. As he went to each room, he saw different geographical places, cultures, and industries in America. He saw little fires kept popping up. The people showing him around would go and stomp out the fires. After a while, the fires started bothering Rick. He and the people with him was about to go outside when they saw a military base outside. He then noticed another small fire and went to stomp it out. After stomping it out, he realized that it had burned through the floor and the subfloor. He looked down under the house and saw that the entire foundation was on fire. Rick wanted to grab his computer and then run for his life. However, he heard the voice of God said, "You don't have time for that. Get your wife and get the fire hose."*

When Rick woke up, he knew this house was about to explode and that it represented America. He knew that wife meant the church, the bride; that the church alone has the fire hose, the water, which represents the Word of God and the truth; and that the only thing which can be done is pour as much water as possible on the foundations [of America] (Roth). The urgent emergency for America scared Rick Joyner whereas, in my dreams, I was not scared of the fires that surrounded me (see dream written earlier in this chapter).

I realized my previous experiences as a victim of spiritual wickedness allowed me to fearlessly face the huge blazing fire in the high-rise building, in my dream. I overcame spiritual attacks from 2008 and beyond, when I had to face multiple levels of demons, one of which was the anti-Christ demon – 666.

I contacted Rick Joyner's ministry and told them about the connection of my dreams about fire with his prophetic dream. Both of our dreams confirmed that high level wickedness is about to destroy the foundation of America. The FBI and the military will not be able to handle it. This is spiritual warfare, not a physical one. Spiritual wickedness is also happening in politics. As seen in the case of Congresswoman Griffords, those who practice spiritual wickedness manipulate innocent people to carry out their works. God revealed this to me in a dream before I saw pictures of her shooter on TV – CNN.

On January 10, 2011, I dreamt, *I was inside my brother, Dave's, house. He was lying on the bed with two small children who he was babysitting. I sat on another bed. My cousin, Letzie, showed up with a few very young children. One of the children, a little girl about three years old, came up to me. I saw that her hair was light blonde. I then noticed that the hair started to fall back from the front and her real hair was exposed. Her real hair was cut very low. I realized she was wearing a wig and it had begun to fall off to the back of her head.*

*Next, I found the same little girl standing between my legs as I sat on the bed. This time her hair was bleached, almost white in color. Her hair was very long and had very small curly braids. I knew I was supposed to comb her hair. I started losing the braids then decided it would take too long. I asked Letzie to lose the braids and then let me know when she was finished so that I could comb the little girl's hair.*

The day after the above dream, at work I was passing by the TV when the CNN news reporter started reporting about the shooting of congresswoman Griffords. I stopped to watch the news. They showed a picture of the shooter with his head clean shaved then previous photos of him with his hair very long and curly. He was a young white man.

Seeing the picture of congresswoman Griffords' shooter reminded me of the baby I dreamt about. In the dream, she first had low-cut hair, covered by a wig; later she was seen with long curly braided hair, which was almost white in color. I realized that as in the dream with the exposure of the little girl's very short cut hair; followed by a change to very long white curly hair; and then me knowing I was supposed to braid her hair but will do it after someone else dealt with it; God was showing me that one of these days, I will have to address the demonic spirit in the young man who shot Congresswoman Griffords. He must first be processed in the natural court of law before God Himself prove it was not him who did it, but the demonic spirit in him which used him to carry out such an act.

Only those who are spiritually equipped can handle deliverance from evil and demonic spirits. The beginning of my spiritual afflictions came with a car accident as a cover, which was caused by an employee of the Israeli Embassy in America. This shows that anyone can be used, innocently, to carry out spiritual wickedness. Eventually, God opened my eyes spiritually so that I could detect when

I was under attack by evil spirits. Unfortunately, most people do not have spiritual discernment.

America needs spiritual warriors of The Almighty God to save her. To do this, they would have to engage in prayer, fasting, praise and worship of God, and vigorously spread the words of God. America needs to call on the Army of the Lord, equipped with God's anointed and appointed soldiers. As children of God, we can overcome what is about to hit America. Those who have experiences overcoming evil in the spiritual realm, will need to be called on, to save America.

I know God is ready for me to expose spiritual wickedness and destroy Satan's kingdom on this earth. Jesus Christ came to earth and died for us so that we can join Him in Heaven, one day. When Jesus was on earth, most of His ministry involved healing and casting out evil and demonic spirits from people. I will be operating under the Spirit of Jesus Christ as I expose spiritual wickedness and destroy Satan's kingdom.

My commission to destroy Satan's kingdom was confirmed at my church on July 24, 2011 when while reading the scripture, Mathew 28:1-20, my spirit reacted to verses 19 and 20. In these verses Jesus Christ is telling me to go and teach all nations to observe all things which He commands and to baptize them in the name of the Trinity – God, Jesus Christ, and the Holy Spirit. Jesus also reassures me He will be with me always, even until the end of the world.

At the end of the service, a visitor who was a pastor from Jamaica said that God told her to tell me to continue working on the documents. I will be successful very soon. I knew God meant His books. This woman did not know me, nor was she told I was writing books for God.

*Chapter 16*

# An Existing Star Is Called

Songs are important in expressing your feelings, desires, concerns, and other emotions that can have little to major impact on others. Coupled with the right kind of music, when songs are sung, they can convey messages to others that can influence their actions, or instill certain emotions in them. It is, therefore, important that you control the types of songs you listen to as much as you can.

As reported by Dreisinger, there are concerns about the lyrics in some types of songs. Lyrics from Snoop Dogg's album, *"Doggystyle"* got the attention of the United States senate due to its pornographic contents. Delores Tucker, the onetime head of the National Congress of Black Women who brought the song to the senate's attention, thought this song was genocidal to children. The Coalition for the Revolution of Corporate Rap group, which includes Al Sharpton, urged record labels to regulate hip hop violence. However, these efforts by well-meaning people don't stop children from listening to hip-hop songs

– good, or bad. As further reported by Dreisinger, Travis Dixon, assistant professor of communication studies at the University of Illinois at Urbana-Champaign indicated that studies show, *"Teens exposed to violent rap expressed greater acceptance of the use of violence."*

The consequence of listening to violent lyrics in songs was brought out in the trial of Ronald Ray Howard for the shooting death of a cop. The influence of hip-hop music came into questioning. Although Ronald Ray Howard grew up in a violent environment and had been involved in many unlawful activities, he claimed it was the angry rap music he was listening to at the time that caused him to pull the trigger (Phillips).

Violent song lyrics increase negative emotions and thoughts that can lead to aggression (Palmer). An online report by the American Psychological Association on violence in songs, indicated that aggression in thoughts and emotions is directly related to the violence in the lyrics. Participants' thoughts and emotions suffered increased aggression when exposed to violent lyrics in songs (American Psychological Association).

The lyrics of heavy metal and rap music and their effects on mood, suicidal ideation, aggression, and stereotyping of adolescents have been of interest to the social science research community. They looked at whether the lyrics in these types of music promote aggression, bigotry, deviant sexual activity, suicide, violence, drug use, and homicide. Palmer cited research from Iowa State University and the Texas Department of Human Services, which "*found that aggressive music lyrics increase aggressive thoughts and feelings, which might perpetuate aggressive behavior and have long-term effects, such as influencing listeners' perceptions of society and contributing to the development of aggressive personalities*" (Palmer para. 2).

The effects of lyrics on behavior can also be seen in a study by Martino et al., which indicated that teenagers who listened to "degrading" song lyrics were more likely to engage in a range of advanced sexual activities. This didn't seem to be true for those who listened to "*non-degrading*" sexual lyrics.

Violence and other suggested social ills in song lyrics are not to be ignored. Well-meaning people or groups, such as Just Think, tried to combat the violence in rap songs through media literacy. They recognize that many young people form identities such as, senses of style, buying habits, morals, and ethics from hip-hop songs, videos and culture (Dreisinger).

Strong influence of songs on people is the desire of songwriters and singing artists so that their works will be profitable. The concern here is whether the songs have positive influence on people. Will the song incite people to violence, hatred, lewdness, sexual immorality, or other undesirable social behavior? Do artists consider the best good of their audience when composing their songs? Will the songs uplift people and society? Are the intended effects of the songs good, or bad, purely profit driven, or considerate of the audience?

We can communicate all sorts of ideas, feelings, desires, concerns, and emotions through songs. They are such powerful communication tools that God Himself desires us to write and sing song to and about Him. Even God Himself can be touched by songs when sang and presented to Him in the right way and with pure intentions. Through songs, we can glorify God, we can praise His name, we can tell Him how much we appreciate Him as our Creator and Father, we can extol His name above all gods, we can testify of our experiences with Him, we can tell others how awesome and mighty He is, we can call on Him to present Himself to us, we can bask in His glory, we can tell Him we love Him, and much more.

God is looking for a new breed of singers who will not only sing His praises and worship Him, but in doing so positively influence those who listen to His songs. God has given me the task of calling out such a singer to do His work. Through a dream and spiritual incident, He allowed me to identify the existing singing artist and allowed me to promise to write songs for Him.

The call for this singer to reach out to people for God is in the following dream:

*I was watching a man film a gospel video. Men and women were dancing as they sang a song. I was enjoying the singing as I watched.*

*After the song finished, I looked behind and saw Mariah Carey and a lady practicing to sing a very beautiful song of praise. They were standing together in a small building on a platform. It was a song I never heard before. The lady kept faltering on one of the verses while Mariah was able to handle it. After a while, the lady turned out to be me. The song gave me a joyful feeling. After the third try, Mariah decided to leave. She was disgusted that I kept faltering while singing.*

*After Mariah left, I found myself singing a song I was familiar with – "I want to thank you Lord with all that is within me. I want to sing the song that you have given me. I want to praise you Lord forever, forever and forever. Lord You have been so good to me"* (Reid---"God Works Through Dreams").

I was not surprise that in the dream I was faltering when singing. I occasionally lose my voice while singing. This dream inspires me to write my own songs of praise to God, when He is ready. I believe one of the songs to be written is the glorious song in the dream, of which I cannot recall one word. At the time of this dream, I was listening to some great gospel music, but the song I heard in the dream is beyond what I ever heard. I am sure that God is faithful to resurrect the words of the dream song when He is ready for me to make it public, based on my promise to Him.

In 2008, while going through spiritual battles, I promised God I would help others who were going through the same experiences I was having and that I would write songs for Him. I heard myself speaking these promises to God from my spirit; in that, I was shocked to hear myself speaking out those words. I knew that I was thinking of writing songs for God because of the dream with the special song. However, my spirit took over and made covenant promises to God about writing songs for Him.

Through many experiences, I realized that God loves songs. I know that the songs I will write for Him will have to be sung by Mariah Carey, or someone of her caliber. I am not saying that God would not appreciate my singing because He demonstrated this to me. On December 14, 2013, I recorded my singing of the song, *Holy, Holy (Worthy Is The Lamb)*. For *"Lord God Almighty Reigns"* I substituted the words, *"Master Adonai Reigns"* and for *"Lord God Almighty"* I substituted the words, *"My God Adonai."* I made the words substitution in the song after He gave a prophecy to my church to call Him by His Hebrew name. He next gave me the name, *"Adonai"* and its meaning of *"Master."* There are many stories related to this, which will be written about in another book.

I managed to completely sing the *"Worthy Is The Lamb* song without my voice cracking, so I added it to the list of songs I play throughout the night from the album, *"The Sound of Heaven,"* by Terry MacAlman. In less than a week after, God allowed me to play the list of songs before I started praying. He then had me crying just before my singing started. Next, He stopped me from praying while the song was playing and had me crying until it ended. This was God's way of letting me know that He had accepted my singing. It showed that God appreciates things done from the heart. Although God showed me His appreciation when I chose to sing for Him, I know that Mariah Carey or, someone of her stature is the one predestined to accomplish that which the songs I will be writing for God is designed to accomplish. I have nieces, who are excellent gospel singers, but I have not even considered them; otherwise, I might be stepping outside the will of God. His special singing assignment is for Mariah Carey.

God confirmed the special calling on Mariah Carey's life during a baptismal service, conducted by my church. He allowed my bishop to call out Mariah Carey's name while he was baptizing a young girl named, Mariah. The call is for Mariah Carey to sing for the glory of God and to use the talent He has given to her to bring souls to Him. God is about to take back the music industry to Himself and He is calling an existing star, Mariah Carey, and a new rare star, myself, to do it for Him. The call of Mariah Carey is part of the story of this book cover, featuring water baptism; a sign of repentance of sin and acceptance of Jesus Christ.

*Chapter 17*

# Giving Tribute to God in Songs

To do justice to God before I even start writing songs for Him, I saw it fit to research the Bible to see how songs were used in Biblical days and what they were about. I found song writing guidance, numerous examples of what people wrote about, and how they used songs. The power of praises to God in songs should not be underestimated. It is a means by which we can get God's attention and it is also a weapon in spiritual warfare. The story of when King Jehoshaphat was faced with the fearsome armies of Moab, Ammon, and the Meunites is a testimony to this.

King Jehoshaphat ordered that a fast (special way of praying to God) be held throughout the country of Judah. The people obeyed and gathered at the temple in Jerusalem. King Jehoshaphat spoke to God in front of the congregation. He called on God in Heaven, the Ruler of kingdoms on earth; he acknowledged the power and might of God, Who no one on earth can withstand; he reminded

God of what He had previously done for the children of Israel and asked God to execute judgment on his enemies.

The Spirit of God, through Jahaziel, told King Jehoshaphat and the congregation not to be afraid because the battle is His, not theirs. God told them to go to battle and He would be there to take care of it. King Jehoshaphat and the congregation bowed down and worship God for His promise. The people trusted God as they went to battle. The battle was won with songs of praises to God, which confused the enemy and caused them to destroy each other, so that King Jehoshaphat's army did not have to fight face to face with them (2 Chronicles 20:1-24). Through praise songs to God, the battle was won. We should also glorify God in songs when we see His wondrous works, as seen in another story about the Israelites.

After God trapped the Egyptian army in the Red Sea and then allowed the water to drown all of them, the Israelites saw the great work of God. They were in awe of God and feared Him. They believed in God and Moses. As tribute to God for His greatness, Moses and the Israelites sang to Him to glorify Him for the victory He gave them. They sang of God's glorious victory. They claimed the Lord as their strength and salvation, declared they will exalt Him, and declared Him to be a Man of war. The Israelites sang of God's Divine act of throwing Pharaoh's army in the Red Sea and drowning them, of the glorious power of the right hand of God, of the wrath of God that destroyed the Egyptians, and of the breath of God that parted the water and made it stand upright as a wall for the Israelites to pass, but released the water to drown the Egyptians. They declared there is no god like the Lord Who is glorious in holiness, and fearful in praises and doing wonders. The Israelites sang of God's guidance of them. They declared that people, including leaders, who hear of the works of God, will be afraid and tremble. Miriam, the prophetess, and all the women played timbrels and danced as they sang to God (Exodus 14:23-30; 15:1-20).

There were other opportunities for the Israelites to sing to God. They sang for water to come forth as they dug a well (Numbers 21:18). After God gave the Israelites victory over Jabin, the king of Canaan, Deborah and Barak sang praises to God (Judges 4, 5). There are other examples of songs in praise and worship of God for deliverance and victory over the enemy.

Praise and worship can be used as a sacrifice to God and for spiritual cleansing. When Hezekaih began to reign over Israel he realized God was angry with the people because they had been unfaithful to God. He ordered cleansing of the temple. He offered burnt offering at the altar along with praise and worship to God, with instruments and the songs of David. After this, the people were cleansed (II Chronicles 29:1-31).

You can sing to God not only when you are in distress, or repenting but also when you are happy with the works He has done in your life (Job 29:13).

David wrote songs about every attribute of God he could think of – His anger, His love, His power, His authority over all things, His glorious majesty, His wondrous works, etc. In song, David described how God deals with the merciful, the upright man, the pure, the wicked, the afflicted, and the haughty. His songs are mostly about the experiences he had with God and experiences he knew of that others had with God. David was a great man of God who used songs to get to the heart of God. It might seem impossible to outdo David in his songs to God, but we can use his examples in writing songs about our experiences with God.

Singing songs is important in worshiping God. According to the Merriam-Webster dictionary, one definition of worship is, *"reverenced offered to a Divine being or supernatural power"* ("Worship"). The Bible teaches us about worship, how to worship God, and the consequence of worshiping other gods. As the Creator of the earth and all that is in it, including you, God desires that we worship Him. You should worship only the Lord God for He is jealous. God is seeking true spiritual worshippers to worship Him in their spirits, as He is a Spirit (John 4:23-24). This is a call for everybody on earth to worship God in a manner like those who live in Heaven.

When you praise God, you are reminded of what He has done, and this sets the stage for worship. The words of God will lead you to worship. You worship God in praise, with His words, in quite time, and in prayer. We should spend quiet time with God and listen to Him as a form of worship. Prayer will get you into worship as you speak to God and listen for Him to speak back to you. It is time to build a true relationship with God. We build casual relationship, then closer relationship, and then intimate relationship with God. Writing songs and singing them to God will help you to get intimate with Him.

*Chapter 18*

# The Joshua Connections

If you should ask me, *"What qualifies you to be conducting commercial business for God?"* I would say, "I got this job because of the anointing God placed on me and my boot camp training in spiritual warfare; conducted by God, Jesus Christ, and the Holy Spirit. However, I come to understand that this is a learn-as-you-go position. There are things of which I am yet to learn. God reveals them just at the time I need to know.

According to a dream I had, I do not know the complete list of what Jesus wants me to have. However, He continues to reveal a little at a time. In many Divine spiritual incidents, He kept pointing me to Joshua. This aroused an interest in me to read the entire book of Joshua in the Bible. I had never read the book of Joshua before until Jesus started directing me to do so.

I often think I should somehow be able to indicate that Jesus Christ is the co-author of my books. After asking me to write books for Him, He brings to me Divine spiritual incidents that I can use to make connections in telling my stories. After all, He never fails me in providing the materials for His books. Here is how Jesus led me to read the book of Joshua so that I can extract relevant information as to how God will be using me in doing His work.

On August 13, 2011, I went to Jamaica's independence celebration in New York. This was organized by a not-for-profit organization. The lady who sang the Jamaican National Anthem and a few other songs was blind.

Later, the blind singer's mother came to my table and passed me a CD. She said she was selling her daughter's CD. I saw that the title of the CD was "*Joshua.*" I opened the CD case and saw the song list. There were only five songs. I was disappointed that it didn't have more songs. I was used to seeing at least ten songs on a CD. When the mother saw that I was looking at the song list and hesitating, she told me that they were gospel songs and the CD cost ten dollars. I did not think the CD was worth that much. However, I decided to buy it to support the singer, only because she was blind. God knows you inside out and therefore knows how to get you to do what He wants you to do.

I later asked my relatives in attendance at the affair – those at my table and those at another table – if the woman sold them the Joshua CD. They all said the woman did not approach them. I thought it was odd that I was the only one she chose to try to sell the CD.

The next day, Sunday August 13, 2011, I decided to listen to the *"Joshua"* CD on my way to church. I took a guest who was staying at my house to church with me. I was late for church, so I took my breakfast with me. When I arrived at my church, I told my guest to go inside and I would first eat my breakfast before I go in. I listened to the last song on the CD, entitled, *"Joshua."* It was about Joshua fighting the battle of Jericho and the wall tumbling down. After the song ended, I went into church (Isaacs).

In church, I saw a white woman and a white man, which was unusual. My bishop later introduced the white woman as, Mary, and said that she and her friend traveled from Poughkeepsie, New York, to come to our church. Mary wanted to be ordained under our ministry and then go out to evangelize. She was gifted in healing and deliverance.

Before the sermon started, Mary went up to share her story. She said she was a chiropractor, who wandered from religion to religion. After her five years old son,

Joshua, died by the hand of witchcraft, she decided to start a *"Joshua Foundation"* to help children who were fatherless. She also started evangelizing.

At one point in her speech, Mary asked everyone to raise their hands in praise to God. She spoke of the different levels of Heaven. She said, as we lift our hand in praise, she would take us up from the second to the third level, which is the throne room of God.

My both hands were raised, as Mary indicated. However, when she spoke about the throne room of God my hands went down and out behind me and I bent over the chair in front of me. I started to cry and groan in my spirit, giving reverence to God. As mentioned in the Bible, our spirits make intercession for us with groaning which cannot be spoken, when we do not know what we should pray for (Romans 8:26). It was as if there was Divine memory about the throne room of God. I could not release myself from the state in which I was. I continued like that until my bishop came and pulled me down to sit. I continued crying, after I sat down.

I remembered that during one of my many spiritual battles, God Himself had taken over. My spirit had spoken out that I was trembling at the throne of God. This incident was confirmation that my spirit had been at the throne room of God before.

I made Divine connection with the story of Mary about her son, Joshua; the Joshua CD I had purchased; the Joshua song I had listened to, just before entering my church (Isaacs); and my hair style. In previous experiences, I had seen where God had used clothing presentation with meaning. I, therefore, related the wall of Jericho in the Joshua song with the way my hair happened to be braided at the time I first listened to it. I had a four-inch round puff at the center of my head with two rings of fat braided fake hair encircling it. The rings in the braid represented the wall of Jericho, as sung about in the Joshua CD (Isaacs).

On August 15, 2011, the Joshua Divine spiritual incidents continued. Before going to bed, I usually read Psalm 91 and say prayers from Charles Capps' book, *God Creative Power Will Work For You*. Since Charles Capps' book was small, I usually insert it back into the Bible at random spots. This time, as I opened the Bible where this book was inserted, I noticed it was placed at the book of Joshua. I normally wouldn't be paying attention to where the small book was located. I knew it was God Who allowed me to pay attention to it, this time.

I decided to read chapters two and three of the book of Joshua where the small book was placed. Chapter two tells of Joshua sending spies into Jericho. Chapter three tells of the crossing of the Jordon River and God's promise to Joshua. *"And the Lord said unto Joshua, this day will I begin to magnify thee in the sight of all Israel, that they may know that, as I was with Moses, so I will be with you"* (Joshua 3:7). I understood it to be that God was showing me He would be with me in carrying out His works, as He was with Moses and Joshua.

On August 21, 2011, I made another connection to the story of Joshua in the Bible. After coming home from church, the guest who was staying at my house gave me a three-piece towel set. Each piece in the set has a positive word written on it – Believe, Praise, and Trust. He said they were in appreciation of what I did for him. I had allowed him to stay at my house when his relatives wouldn't.

My daughter, Sonia, then took me into the bathroom and showed me a gift set of toothbrush holder, soap dish, and garbage container – each has a positive word written on it. Sonia then showed me the shower curtain she had hung up. This was a part of the bathroom gift set the guest had bought for me. The shower curtain has words written all over it. One immediately caught my eyes. The topic is

"*Serve*" and it reads, "*But as for me and my house, we will serve the Lord – Joshua 24:15.*"

This spiritual incident with words from the book of Joshua on the shower curtain being drawn to my eyes was the latest in the series of Joshua connection God was making with me. I told Sonia and my guest of how God was drawing me to pay attention to the story of Joshua in the Bible.

On August 28, 2011, while in Georgia, I had the opportunity to speak to my friend, Donna, about the Divine spiritual incidents leading me to the book of Joshua. She told me she recently had an experience in which she met a male angel who told her God was going to use her like Moses. I knew she was an angel of God sent down to help people, according to a dream I had. What she said to me confirmed what I had in my spirit – God was going to use me like He used Joshua in the Bible.

It came to my spirit that God wanted me to find materials from the book of Joshua, which would be relevant to what I was writing about in the manuscript for this book. I decided to explore the entire book of Joshua, so I would not miss what God was showing me.

The book of Joshua tells the story of the Israelite invasion of Canaan under the leadership of Joshua, the successor of Moses. Major events in this book include the crossing of the Jordon River, the fall of Jericho, the battle at Ai, and the renewal of the covenant between God and the Israelites. In reviewing the entire book of Joshua, I extracted some of his stories I believe God wanted me to pay attention to, based on how He will be using me.

God told Joshua that no one would defeat him as long as he lives. God would never abandon Joshua, but would be with him always. He told Joshua to be determined, confident, not discouraged, and to obey the law Moses gave him. If Joshua did not neglect any part of it, he would always be successful. God told Joshua to go and take the land He had given to the Israelites, without fear. Joshua had soldiers to help execute the command of God. The consequence to those who disobeyed Joshua was death. The people of Canaan were terrified of the Israelites.

The Ark of the Covenant of God played a key role in the execution of God's work with the Israelites. God told Joshua He would make people realize Joshua was a great man and they would honor him. People would know God was with Joshua as He was with Moses. Joshua told the Israelites they would drive out the Canaanites, the Hittites, the Hivites, the Perizzites, the Girgashites, the Amorites, and the Jebusites.

Under the leadership of Joshua, the Israelites crossed the Jordon River with God doing His wondrous works through priests and the Ark of His Covenant. The Amorite kings and Canaanite kings heard that God had dried up the Jordan River until the people of Israel crossed it and they became afraid.

It was the new generation of freshly circumcised Israelite men who could fight and take over the land of Canaan. After the circumcision, God declared He had removed the disgrace of the Israelites being enslaved by the Egyptians.

Joshua met the commander of God's army and God allowed the Israelites to capture Jericho simply by marching around it for seven days with the Ark of the Covenant, blowing trumpet, and shouting. On the seventh day the Israelites took Jericho and destroyed everything except the prostitute, Rahab, and her family. God was with Joshua, and his fame spread throughout the country.

God yet again displayed His might in battle by simply using the pointing of sword and the tactic of retreat to capture Ai for the Israelites. The people of Gibeon befriended Joshua under false pretense because they feared him. Joshua fell for the trick because he did not consult with God. After the friendship was formed and the city of

Ai captured, king Adonizedek of Jerusalem formed a coalition with neighboring kings to attack Gibeon.

God sent Joshua and his army to help Gibeon and told Joshua He has given him the victory and he should not be afraid. The Amorites panicked at the sight of the Israelites and fled. The Lord rained down hailstones as they fled and more of them were killed by hail stones than by the hands of the Israelites.

God allowed Joshua to command the sun to stand still over Gibeon and the moon to stop over Aijalon Valley until the Israelites finished conquering their enemies. The sun stood still in the middle of the sky and did not go down for a whole day. Never before, and never since, has there been a day like it, when the Lord obeyed a human being. The Lord obeyed Joshua and fought on Israel's side. Joshua and the men of Israel slaughtered the Amorites, and no one dared to speak against the Israelites.

Joshua captured Makkedah, Libnah, Lachish, Gezer, Eglon, Hebron, and Debir. He conquered the entire land by defeating one country after the other and putting all the inhabitants to death, just as the Lord God of Israel had commanded. Joshua was able to conquer them all because God was fighting for Israel.

The kings of Hazor, Madon, Shimron, and Achshaph; the Amorites, Hittites, Perizzites, Jebusites, and Hivites joined together against the Israelites, resulting in an army that was like the sand on the seashore and having many horses and chariots. The Lord told Joshua not to be afraid of them because the next day He would kill them all for Israel. God told Joshua to cripple their horses and burn their chariots.

The next day the Israelites fought against the joint army and when they were done, all of their enemies were killed, and their cities burned. Joshua crippled their horses and burned their chariots as the Lord had commanded. The only city that made peace with the Israelites was Gibeon, where the Hivites lived. All other cities were conquered in battle. God had made them determined to fight the Israelites so that they could be condemned to total destruction and all would be killed without mercy. This was what the Lord commanded Moses. Thirty-one kings were defeated by the Israelites.

God had been fighting for the Israelites and taking away the possessions of other nations. Because the Israelites were faithful to God He allowed them to overtake great and powerful nations. However, if they disobey the laws of Moses; associate with people who were left among them; vow to, or worship other gods; or intermarry with other nations; God would no longer give them the victory and they would be in danger of their enemies. The danger would exist for the Israelites until none of them remained in the land which God gave them.

As God has kept his promise to the Israelites, so He would carry out His threats. Joshua warned that if the Israelites did not keep the covenant, which God made with them, and if they worship other gods, then God would get angry and punish them. They would all have to leave the land God gave them.

Joshua told the Israelites to honor and serve God sincerely and faithfully. They were to get rid of the gods their ancestors used to worship and serve only the Lord God. The Israelites were to choose who they would serve – the gods their ancestors worshiped in Mesopotamia, the gods of the Amorites, or the Lord God. Joshua declared that he and his family would serve the Lord God.

Throughout the book of Joshua I see where God fiercely defended a nation with which He made a covenant (Joshua 7:11). He removed their disgrace of slavery in Egypt (Joshua 5:7-9), fought mightily in unconventional ways to allow them to have victory over their enemies (Joshua 2:10), and allowed other nations to fear them when they saw He was their defense (Joshua 9:3-18). I learned that I should always consult with God before doing any business on His company's behalf. What I am doing for God will remove the disgrace of slavery from the black race, like what the circumcision of the new generation did for the Israelites' enslavement in Egypt. I am to serve God sincerely and faithfully.

I know God constantly pointed me to the book of Joshua to reassure me that the same way he defended the children of Israel He will defend me as He uses me to carry out His works through His company – Works Of Trinity, LLC.

I have taken you through a lot of connections God made with me and the Biblical Joshua, who lead the Israelites to the Promised Land. However, here is one last one. When doing my final edit of this book's manuscript, I recognized that God used the Joshua's CD with five songs to confirm my thought of cutting a CD with the songs I sung for Him. my CD also has five songs – one about His name Adonai, with the meaning of Master; one alleluia song to reverse the works of the enemy; one which shows my stance in God; and two which I had to use in the battle to unseat the 666 demon that wanted to take over my church. This CD was produced for God, which established a way of taking back the music industry for Him.

*Chapter 19*

# Joshua's Anointing

I can never know what God will do next, but I did conclude He was going to use me as He used Joshua. After God got me to pay full attention to the story of Joshua in the Bible and I read all the chapters, He took the next step. As usual, God uses the church which I attend to do His works and make divide connections in my life.

My church had planned a week of convention in the last week of August 2011 with Bishop Goldstein from Florida as special guest speaker. His flight was delayed because of the unusual occurrence of hurricane Irene in the tri-state area. The convention extended to two weeks and continued with Bishop Goldstein from September 4, 2011 onwards. I could see that he was a highly anointed man of God. The first night he preached, I had never witnessed so many people filled with the Holy Spirit, in the church.

The second night I went to the convention early. My bishop came to me and told me that he found a tape in his office with my name on it. I went to look and saw that it was the taping of an exhortation of God I did a year ago at our Ladies' Convention in October 2010. I told him to keep it and get the DVD done for me. My bishop was supposed to convert it to DVD for me, but both of us forgot about it.

Bishop Goldstein came a little late. Before he started the sermon, he related his experience at his church when he was bored and sleepy, while preaching. He said that in his most boring sermon, the glory of God showed up. In that, the cross in front of him lighted up and made flashes of light across the room. People got scared.

As Bishop Goldstein continued talking, my spirit was moved by what he was relating. I found myself fighting evil spirit to do what God wanted me to do. When Bishop Goldstein spoke about Jesus I felt my hands became outstretched firmly across the chairs and my head bowed slightly, as when Jesus' picture is seen on the cross. All this time, my eyes were closed. I groaned in my spirit as Bishop Goldstein continued to speak. It was as if I was agonizing over the cross. I continued like this for a while.

My body's position was released after a while. Bishop Goldstein called people to the altar. I went to the altar. He asked people to lift their hands. He asked for a glimpse of the glory of Jesus. After that, he said Jesus would show Himself. My spirit responded to what he was saying, and I made angelic movements with my hands outstretched.

The Divine spiritual incidents of me responding to the cross of Jesus, while under spiritual attack; and my display of the presence of Jesus were related to the sudden discovery of my tape by my bishop, after forgetting about it for nearly a year. I had my name on the tape and the title, God's Exhortation. God brought it to my attention, so I would know He was going to allow me to act out exhortations of Jesus. I came to realize God has totally unexpected ways of making Divine connections, you just must be in tuned with Him to recognize when He is working. He has His own way of differentiating His work from that of Satan, even when Satan tries to get in the middle of His work.

On September 7, 2011, I went to convention at church, in the evening. The convention continued with Bishop Goldstein as the guest preacher. While preaching he said, *"Somebody's life is not going to be the same as you know it because the anointing is going to fall on you. I came to deliver a message. God sent me here to anoint an Elijah. I don't know if it is a man or a woman. God says He is going to change the way things are. Revival can spring up from anywhere. God knows the very place where you were going to sit. There is a price to pay. The anointing attracts the devil."*

After preaching for a while, Bishop Goldstein said God Himself was about to make an altar call. I was one of many people who responded to God's altar call. However, my response was different from the others. I had my left hand outstretched in the air towards Heaven, in a fist, and my right hand at my heart, in a fist, as I sat in my chair. I was groaning in my spirit and continued in this state for a while. Others who heeded the altar call were on the ground and crying out in The Holy Spirit.

I often use my hands in response to God. The Bible often references the hand of God, so there must be a good reason for me using my hands in response to the movement of The Holy Spirit in me.

I went to my church's convention on September 8, 2011. Bishop Goldstein continued to be the guest preacher. He said many things which I could relate to a man I know. I felt in my spirit that I should invite him to come the next day because it would be the last day of the convention. I invited him, and he said he would try to make it after work.

On September 9, 2011, while at work, my supervisor called me and another teammate to follow him to a project manager to participate in a discussion about the project on which we were working. My supervisor wanted to sort out the latest information on proposed changes. At one point in the discussion, I started rubbing both my eyes vigorously for no apparent reason. After I was done, the project manager commented to my supervisor on the situation they were trying to sort out. She said, *"I see not, I speak not, and I hear not."* I knew I was supposed to pay attention to her comment since it followed the unusual itching of my eyes.

In the evening, I went to the last day of convention at my church. Again, Bishop Goldstein was the guest preacher. Early in his preaching, he was calling out for a man who God wanted to come forward. He spent about fifteen minutes, just calling the man to come forward. No one went forward. I knew Bishop Goldstein was calling for the man I invited to the convention, but he did not show up.

After a while, Bishop Goldstein got tired of calling for *"the man"* God wanted. He told everyone to get up and hug seven people to show love and say, *"Jesus is Lord and the devil is a liar."* He then said to hug seven more people.

Bishop Goldstein spoke some things that related to me. However, the key things he spoke of, which got my attention were about the eyes, ears, and mouth. I was reminded of the incident with the project manager at work, earlier in the day. Although my spirit did not get moved while I was sitting and Bishop Goldstein was preaching, I went up to the altar when he said, *"Anyone who thinks I might be talking to you, come to the altar."*

Bishop Goldstein continued preaching after many of us went up and stood at the altar. He prayed for some people in between preaching. He said something that caused me to cry out in the spirit. I then bowed my head and placed both of my hands – in fists – at the front of my face. I stayed like this at the altar, as if waiting for something else.

Bishop Goldstein spoke that the anointing of Joshua was there. As he said this, my spirit was moved, and I received the anointing with both hands in fists and stretched upwards to Heaven, in front of me. While receiving the anointing, I was thinking that the man I invited to church was not there to receive this anointing. I knew I was taking it on his behalf.

After the service, I gave a church member a ride to her house. She told me that The Holy Spirit came upon one woman while Bishop Goldstein was preaching. She fell to the ground and while she was on the ground, her underwear was exposed. A church member had to quickly get a sheet to cover up the woman. I did not know that God allowed me to hear about this for a reason.

God has unique ways of confirming things to me. I can never guess how He will do it. His confirmation of the anointing of Joshua was no different. He used a water situation in my basement – His office – to connect to a dream He gave to my sister, Ruth, which confirmed the Joshua anointing.

On September 10, 2011, there was a little water in the middle of my basement due to heavy rain for many days. It was there for a few days since I did not have the time to dry it up. I finally found the time to mop up the water. I was disappointed that after fixing the basement as an office for God I was getting water in. However, I could not see where it was coming from.

After I finished mopping up the water, I went into the kitchen and the phone rang. It was Ruth. She said she was calling to tell me about her dream. She dreamt, *she went back to her old office to move out some things and do some cleaning up. She noticed water on the floor that came in because of snow. She cleaned under the desk and saw a lot of dust. She next started praising God with her hands in the air. She was so much into praising God that all her clothes fell off and her vagina was exposed. This did not stop her from continuing to praise God.*

I immediately told Ruth of the anointing incident at church with my hand outstretched to Heaven and the lady's underwear being exposed when she got filled with The Holy Spirit, while the anointing was taking place.

I knew this was confirmation from God of me being fully exposed to all about what He has anointed me to do for Him; through the business He allowed me to establish for Him, in my basement. He had sent Bishop Goldstein to my church to pass on the anointing of Joshua, leader of the Israelites, to me. Somehow, Ruth is also connected to this anointing.

## Discovery of Joshua, The Priest/BRANCH

I was hesitant to write about God using me to do exhortation of Jesus at my church because I had to fight a demonic spirit before I could do it. I wrote of it to honor God because He had alerted me that He would be using me to do His exhortation. He allowed my bishop to discover the tape of the exhortation I did for Him, previously, just before the start of the church service. Satan was trying to prevent me from doing what God wanted me to do. In making the bold decision to write about my exhortation of

Jesus Christ, God lead me to connect Moses' and Joshua's leadership of the children of Israel and the use of my hands, while receiving His anointing.

I decided to research the Bible for further information about God's use of hand. I started from the beginning of the Old Testament. Even though I found many references to *"hand,"* I did not stop looking because I knew in my spirit I did not find what I was looking for, although I did not know what it was. In Zechariah chapter three, I found what I knew I was supposed to incorporate into my writing. It is where Satan was standing at the right *"hand"* of Joshua, the high priest, to create problem for him. God used the story of Joshua, the priest, who presented himself in filthy clothes to the angel of the Lord while Satan stood by to give trouble, to confirm to me that in my experience, I too, had to fight and overcome Satan to do His work. I was encouraged by the story of Joshua, the high priest.

In a vision, Zechariah saw Joshua, the high priest, standing before the angel of the Lord. Satan was standing at the right hand of Joshua to cause him trouble. The angel of the Lord reprimanded Satan and told him Joshua was one who had been through the fire.

Joshua had on filthy clothing and the angel told those who were with him to remove Joshua's filthy clothes.

He then told Joshua he had removed his sins and will give him new clothing. Joshua was given new headdress and clothing to put on. The angel told Joshua that God said if he obeyed God, did the things God told him to do, Joshua would be in command of God's house, and Joshua would be given the same privilege as the angels who were in His presence. God called Joshua His servant – the BRANCH and promised to reveal him. God laid a seven-sided (heptagon) stone before Joshua and promised He would write on it and remove the sins of the land in one day. When that day comes, everyone will invite his neighbor under the vineyard and fig tree (Zechariah 3:1-10).

Joshua, the high priest and son of Josedech, was again a figure in another of Zechariah's vision. The Lord told Zechariah to make crowns of silver and gold and put them on Joshua's head. Zechariah should tell Joshua he was the branch that would arise and build the temple of God. Joshua would be honored for doing this. He would rule like a king but would be a priest on this throne. There would be peace between both roles. The crowns would be a memorial in the Lords temple in honor of the people who made them – Helem, Tobijah, Jedaiah, and Hen. People from far would come to help build the temple of the Lord. All this would happen if Joshua diligently obeyed the Lord (Zechariah 6:11-15).

After God led me to discover about the other Joshua, the high priest, and I incorporated it into my writing, He allowed my niece, Petrona, to provide confirmation that He has also given me the anointing of Joshua, the priest.

On December 17, 2011, Petrona told me she dreamt, *she was in my basement with her family. She was lying on a bed. Her daughter, Zedon, jumped on the bed. The bed overturned with Petrona. She dropped into a basement below the one she was in. She was surprised there was another basement beneath that one. The bottom basement was much bigger than the top one. It had just opened space. The walls were finished, and it was looking very good. However, the flooring was dirt, not concrete. It looked as if there was water on the floor, but it was already cleaned up.*

*Petrona felt like this basement was a place where you could go and relax and find peace of mind. She said, "How comes Jenness has this big basement. Why doesn't she fix it?" Petrona then went upstairs and saw me. She said to me, "Why don't you fix up the big basement you have down there?" I replied, "Yes, I am going to fix it and give it to Sonia."*

As compared to Joshua, the branch, I was commissioned by God to fix my basement as His business office; I had two guys coming from far to do the work and after they finished, I could feel the glory of God in it for a very long time.

For the priestly anointing of the Joshua who will arise and build His temple, God used Petrona to confirm this just after I searched the Bible and gotten information on this Joshua. In Petrona's dream, God allowed her to speak to me about fixing up the basement, which I refer to as God's office. Also, in this dream, God used the symbol of water in His office, so I could connect this dream to that of Ruth's – the one that confirmed the first Joshua's anointing. The connection in both dreams is the incident of me mopping up water in God's office just before hearing Ruth's dream involving water while she was cleaning out her office at work and Petrona's dream having freshly mopped floor with the indication that there was water in the basement.

I was also able to connect Sonia in Petrona's dream to me giving her the task of decorating the living and dining room area (other basement in the dream) for my family's Christmas party. In Petrona's dream, I told her I would fix the basement and give it to Sonia. Instead, I had Sonia doing the fixing up for Christmas dinner on December 24, 2011.

I told Sonia to get a real Christmas tree, but instead she bought a fake one. We had a large opened space (as in Petrona's dream) to fit the forty-two guests since there were no walls between the living room and dining room. The flooring was wood. This scene fitted the wide opened bottom basement in Petrona's dream and the different flooring of wood and concrete (dirt flooring in the dream).

During the Christmas party, one of my neighbors knocked on my door to complain that a car was parked too close to her driveway. I was able to relate the unexpected arrival of my neighbor to the story of Joshua, the branch. God had told Joshua, the priest, that in one day He would remove the sin of the land and everyone would invite his neighbor to enjoy that day under the vineyard and fig tree (Zechariah 3:9-10).

I knew God wanted me to have the Christmas dinner at my house and to invite some family members who had drifted apart. It was here that God created a peaceful and glorious atmosphere; one which I had never experienced at any previous celebrations. I could tell that

God's presence was with us. He had removed barriers within the family. The unexpected arrival of the curious neighbor was just a Divine spiritual incident to confirm what is written about neighbor been invited to the vineyard (my house) on that special day. Before I step out into doing business for God, my family must come together and be united.

Whenever God puts information in my spirit He always has some way of confirming it so that I can differentiate my own thoughts from what He instills in me. The anointing of Joshua, the branch, the high priest, is no exception.

*Chapter 20*

# Aftermath of the Anointing

As Bishop Goldstein mentioned during the convention at my church, the anointing does attract the devil. The devil will try to prevent the anointing from manifesting. Even Jesus' anointing was challenged by the devil (Satan), in the wilderness (Matthew 4:1). Jesus Christ was prophesied to be the servant of God Who used wisdom in his dealings; would be highly exalted; had a disfigured faced that looked less than human; his works would affect many nations, making rulers speechless when they see and understand what he speaks of (Isaiah 52:13-15).

Jesus Christ was also prophesied to be a servant who grew as a tender plant, rooted in a dry ground. Although He was not handsome that people would desire Him, He would take on our sins and sacrifice Himself for us; He would be despised, rejected, plagued with suffering and grief, and ignored. Though innocent; He was punished for our sins and by his stripes, we were healed. Because of

*Aftermath of the Anointing*

the great sacrifice Jesus made for us, He was given a place of honor with God (Isaiah 53:1-5). Jesus was challenged by the devil because he knew the purpose for Jesus coming to earth. He was trying to prevent Jesus from fulfilling His purpose.

I know the devil has his ways of finding out God's purpose for your life. When he discovered mine, I too was in for a fight with him. I had to defend my anointing. This is the story of my challenges and triumphs.

Those who the devil uses in executing his work have ways of knowing what you have already overcome and will therefore seek new ways to defeat you. They will even use innocent people to get at you – especially those who are close to you. The sad thing is that people are not aware when they are being used in executing the devil's work. In my case, it was my daughter who was innocently used against me.

On September 7, 2011, my daughter, Sonia, came back from a trip to Florida. She called me while I was at work. I could feel evil sensation going into my ears and mouth as I held my cell phone to my ears. I realized she was being used to send evil spirits against me. Later I had a dream that indicated the quantity of evil venom that came back with Sonia from Florida.

## Aftermath of the Anointing

On September 11, 2011, I dreamt that, *Sonia and I were getting a ride with my bishop. He stopped on the road to let us out of the car. I saw four large, long plastic bottles filled with clear liquid and a smaller one; also with clear liquid. I knew they belonged to Sonia.*

*The dream changed scene. I found myself dusting off my ottoman. I knew I was supposed to be getting ready to go to church, but I wanted to finish the cleaning first. When I was finished, I saw that church was almost over and people were about to leave.*

After I woke up I decided to go and sit in the computer room to do online banking. As I sat in the chair, I could feel the presence of evil. I realized the evil spirit I encountered in Sonia's room the day before and chased out had come to the computer room. I started doing spiritual battle with the evil spirit. I then opened the closest window and let it out.

The encounter with evil spirit caused me to be late for church. As I parked my car on the road next to the church, I could feel the presence of evil. I started doing spiritual battle while sitting in the car until I got rid of it. I seemed like the evil spirit I let out of my house had gone into the car. I finally got out of the car and as I turned the corner, I saw a man on a very tall ladder, resting on top of the roof of the church. I was feeling somewhat concerned that they were working on the roof while church was in session. However, I remembered the constant leaking of water into one of the bathrooms whenever rain falls.

By the time I went into the church, the service had long started. At one point during the sermon, my bishop said demons were placed in a plastic bag and thrown on the top of the church's roof to try and destroy the church. The demons would come down the crack in the roof and into the church when no one was around. As my bishop spoke about the roof of the church, my spirit cried out and I held my head with both hands for a while repeating, "*Oh my God. My God.*"

After church, I picked up Sonia from Petra and felt the presence of evil spirits. I realized it was the dye in her hair which she came back with from Florida that was used to send evil spirits against me. Her hair was dyed purple with beige near the root. About a month ago, Kristal had two similar dreams that pointed to something Sonia was involved in. In the first dream, *a man was trying to tell Kristal that Sonia was involved in something but was not able to do so because Sonia was close to him.* In the second dream, *the same man was talking to Kristal about Sonia. He spoke to her about evil spirit.*

At the time of hearing about these dreams, I explained to both my daughters that it could be someone Sonia was associated with who was involved in something evil. She didn't have to be aware of this. After I became aware that whosoever dyed Sonia's hair in Florida had used her hair in some evil way, I tried to get her to re-dye it to get out whatever was placed in it. She got offended and left the house for a very long time. Although she was upset with me she eventually re-dyed her hair several times to get rid of that blend of dyes.

Days later when I was braiding Sonia's hair, I saw that a small piece of her hair was cut out. I knew it was not like that before she went to Florida because I was constantly braiding her hair. The hairdresser she went to there must have taken out a piece of her hair to use against me.

As it turned out, Sonia was not the only innocent person used by the devil to challenge me. On September 12, 2011, my co-worker, Boland, came to me twice to ask for my headset. He checked it to compare with what he was about to order. The second time after he put it back on my desk, I felt that it was heavily laced with evil spirit. I realized he was also being used to get to me since we were close. After I went home, I had to cast out evil spirit from myself in the bathroom by using olive oil and running water on my hands.

Later, Sonia came from school and returned my headband she had borrowed. She put it in the cabinet drawer. After she left, I touched it and felt it was laced with evil spirit. I started washing it with a bar soap, doing hand movements, as directed by The Holy Spirit, until nothing was left of the soap.

Not long after dealing with the evil spirit transferred from Sonia's head to my headband, I was by the house phone when it rang once. I pressed the speaker and heard someone on the other end. Sonia had picked up the phone at the first ring as if she had expected the call. I could immediately sense the force of evil spirits being transmitted. I started fighting fiercely. The fight lasted about ten minutes. After it ended, I read Psalm 91. At verse 14, I got stuck on the words, "*I will deliver him.*" I repeated those words about fifty times.

On September 13, 2011, in the morning, Sonia took the car and ran an errand. When she returned the car key, I got the sensation of evil spirits being on the key as I touched it.

Once again, I had to go to the bathroom to cast out demons. This demon was more stubborn than the others. As before, I used running water while I washed my hands with bar soap in circular and straight motions. Later, I spoke out, "*I love Jesus.*" The demon responded and repeated several times, "*You love Jesus?*" I then declared, "*Jesus is my husband.*" The demon responded and repeated several times, "*Jesus is your husband?*" I next put some soapy water in my mouth and swirl it around. This irritated it and it left me.

Later I went downstairs and saw a text message on my cell phone from my ex-husband. He typed, "*Today marks the 1st year. Today is also our daughter's birthday. I hope it is happy anniversary for you.*" I did not remember it was Kristal's birthday. I called Kristal and wished her happy birthday.

Later I went to Walgreen's pharmacy to get eucalyptus oil. Mitty was at my house and had advised me to use a few drops of it in honey and lime for the severe sore throat I had. I knew this severe sore throat was due to the demonic attacks and the fights I was engaged in.

There was no eucalyptus oil at the pharmacy, so I got cough candy that contained it. As I stood by the register, I was repeating under my breath, "*Go in the name of Jesus,*" because I realized I had picked up more demons after touching my handbag and cell phone. My eyes were drawn to a wooden pendant around the cashier's neck. It was a carving of Jesus' head. I knew it was Jesus who allowed me to notice it to reassure me of His presence with me.

The most intense part of the vicious evil spirit attacks which was mostly electronic was from September 7, 2011 to October 10, 2011. I could tell that the focus of the new onslaught of evil spirit attacks was my head, face, and ears. At one point, I could feel when the evil venom was seeping through my head, face, and ears. I could feel when the attacks were coming through the phones, whether I used the headset at work, the regular handset at work, or my cell phone. I felt the evil spirit sensation over my house phone for a short time. However, the focus of the attack was over my cell phone and my phone at work.

At one point, the evil spirit attack got so intense I had to stop carrying around my cell phone for a few days. I could feel a slight metallic taste in my mouth and smell metallic fragrance. I asked Kristal to change my voice message to tell callers I was unable to answer the phone and they should text me, if they could. My hearing got tender from answering my cell phone and work phone. The attack using my house phone was very brief. The worst case of my cell phone attack was when Sonia called me.

Demons continued to pursue me at home, on the road, and at work. September 15, 2011 was a day of revelation from some of the demons about themselves. Some of them got verbal. Their reactions were triggered by different things. For one of them the trigger was the words from a CD I was playing on my way to work. It was all about *"fire"* – God calling on His children to arise with fire in their hands and feet (Lewis). The demon started repeating the words, *"fire, Jesus, oh my God"* and then started making groaning noises.

I had to stop at a shopping mall and struggle with it to leave me. I was able to get it to tell me who sent it. It told me Teddy sent it to kill *"the anointed"*; it didn't like *"the anointed;"* it didn't like me; it was going back to kill him; he couldn't conquer it; I would hear about it when it killed him; and God said it should kill him. After doing all that talking, it asked me to let it go. I released the demon and then continued to work.

The next verbal exposure of a demon was initiated by me in a parking lot. I demanded it to get out in the name of Jesus and asked it who sent it. It told me it was not supposed to talk. It was very reluctant in giving its name and was trying to use delay tactic, by stammering. In the middle of this, my cell phone rang. This triggered the demon to speak out. It said its name was phone; it was sent by Afrah. It spelt out the name A F R A H. I told it not to lie. It responded that it was Frank and Teddy who sent it. They told it to kill me when the phone rings. I told it to go back to them. It told me it was not going; it didn't like them.

Later at home, I demanded the phone demon to get out in the name of God, in the name of Jesus, and in the name of The Holy Spirit. It responded by asking God why He had to take me away. It said it felt ashamed to go back. It was never defeated. It said God won't allow it to kill me. It said it loved me and wanted to stay with me. I told it to go in the name of Jesus. It responded by telling Jesus that it was confused and didn't know what to do.

Another exposure of one kind of demon I dealt with was triggered by a song I was playing on my way to work. The lyric is, *"devil hafi run wen Jesus cum,"* translated as, *"devil has to run when Jesus comes."* The demon repeated the words in an angry tone. I insisted it should tell me who sent it. It hesitated for a long time and it was only after I parked my car it said that Haka sent it. It spelt the name twice, H A K A.

On October 10, 2011, at work, my manager stopped by and saw the drawing on my desk which was circles within the outline of a headset. The day I had gotten the headset at work, I returned to my desk and saw the drawing of a headset on it. I was annoyed by it. I later realized the headset was being used as one way of attacking me with evil spirit. I tried several ways to get rid of the drawing but couldn't do so completely. In frustration, I drew circles within it.

My manager asked me what the drawing was. I told her how it came about and told her of my efforts to get rid of it. She told me I made it worst. After she said that, I could smell the metallic fragrance of evil spirit rising from the headset drawing on my desk. After this, the headache I was having for four days started to go away. I realized God allowed my manager to find out about the drawing so that the evil spirit would leave.

Another form of attack used to challenge my anointing was interference with my food. After Kristal told me of a dream she had of *asking Sonia why she ate out the food and then felt a strange sickening feeling in her heart*, I knew she had encountered familiar evil spirit that was messing with our food.

I went to the kitchen to say my prayers. While saying my prayers close to one of the kitchen cupboards, the demon reacted when I mentioned the words, *"I don't desire to eat so much....*" It started questioning, "*You don't desire to eat so much?*" I then tried to send it away, but it was very stubborn. I finally decided to take two coins and go to the side door. I hurled the coins across the edging by the roadside and told the demon to go in the name of Jesus.

I went upstairs to my room. I was surprised to see a leaf from the edging lying beside my bed. I knew this was the work of the demon that was sent against me. I got a plastic bag from the bathroom and poured some Epsom salt and anointed olive oil into it. I then used the plastic bag to take up the leaf and threw it outside.

I thank God, He had enabled me to overcome the challenges Satan presented to me in defending my anointing. Satan was an anointed cherub in Heaven who was highly decorated with gems of every kind and every stringed instrument. He had led the worship of God in Heaven. However, he got corrupted because of his beauty, wisdom in conducting business, and musical ability. He became proud and coveted the worship that was given to God, a worship that was orchestrated through him. He desired to be worshipped and he felt that with all that musical ability, he should be the one to be worshipped.

Satan sought and corrupted one third of the lesser angels who was in awe of his beauty and musical ability.

He planned to overthrow God and take his throne (Ezekiel 28:2-19). Now, because of the punishment Satan got from God, he is always seeking to corrupt us, so we too would be in trouble with God. The devil wants to hinder us from carrying out the work God destined for us. He will always seek to challenge your anointing and corrupt you, like what he did to a third of the angels in Heaven.

To qualify to manage God's business, I had to face Satan and overcome him. Although Satan was involved in commerce (Ezekiel 28:16), the concept of God going corporate must be a surprise to him and one that will leave him confused – just like one of the demons that attacked me was confused.

Chapter 21
# The Mighty Hands of God

The unique ways I used my hands for the Elijah anointing (during God's altar call) and for the Joshua anointing caused me to wonder what was so special about the hands. To get some idea as to why God uses my hands so much when I am taken over by the Holy Spirit, I researched "*hand*" in the Bible. I found that the hand of God is referenced mainly – in delivering people from their distresses, in Him working through the hand of His anointed, in Him chastising people for wrongs they have done, in displaying His power, and in blessing people.

In deliverance, God stretched out His hand against Egypt to deliver the Israelites from slavery (Exodus 3:20; 9:15). The hand of God delivered the Israelites from their enemy (Ezra 8:31; Nehemiah 9:27). The strong hand of God is effective in deliverance (Nehemiah 1:10).

In the use of His anointed, the most famous stories referenced are those of Moses, Aaron, and Joshua. God used the hands of Moses and Aaron with a rod to turn the river into blood and destroy the fish in it and to turn other waters into blood (Exodus 7:17-25). He used the hand of Moses to stretch towards Heaven and bring down hail on the Egyptian and their animals and crops (Exodus 9:22), to bring locust and darkness on Egypt (Exodus 10:12; 10:21-22), and to stretch across the sea to part it for safe travel of the Israelites, and then to gather it together after the Israelites crossed safely (Exodus 14:16-27). God gave great power to the hands of Moses to bring about deliverance to the Israelites (Exodus 13:3; 13:9; 13:14-16) and punishment to the Egyptians.

God used Joshua's hand with a spear to stretch and conquer Ai (Joshua 8:18-19; 8:26). The hand of God stands against your enemy to protect you (I Samuel 7:13).

There are many references of God using His hand to chastise people and even entire cities because of their disobedience and wrongdoing. God used His hand to shake up kingdoms as He commanded the destruction of the stronghold in the city of Tyre (Isaiah 23:8-11). The hand of God destroyed the city of the Philistines and the false god people worshiped; and He used His hand to bring disease on them (I Samuel 5:1-11; 6:5). The mighty hand of God caused hail, storm, and flood (Isaiah 28:2).

When God's hand is against you for evil you have done, it will bring you distress (Judges 2:15; I Samuel 5:6-7; Psalm 32:4; 39:10; Isaiah 5:25; 9:12; 9:17; 40:2). If you rebel against God and disobey Him then His hand will be against you (I Samuel 12:15). God will stretch out His hand to destroy you when He is tired of repenting about your sinful ways (Jeremiah 15:6; Lamentations 2:4; 2:8; Ezekiel 14:13; 16:27). God will allow you to know Him by the might of His hand (Jeremiah 16:21). God fights with an outstretched hand in anger, fury, and wrath (Jeremiah 21:5). God lifted His hand against Israel in the wilderness in anger because they rebelled against Him with their idol worship and complaints. He did not destroy them in the wilderness because it would bring shame to His name after He brought them out of Egypt with such show of His power, through the hands of Moses and Aaron. Instead, God scatter the Israelites all over the world (Ezekiel 20:13-23).

With the power of His hand, God will gather the children of Israel from all over the world and bring them to Israel where He will deal with them face to face. He will purge the rebels from among the Israelites, so that they do not enter Israel. They will know that He is the Lord. God will bring the Israelites back into the land of Israel that He had used His hand to give to them. The Israelites will remember their evil ways and know that the Lord their God will work with them to protect His name and not deal with them according to what they deserve (Ezekiel 20:38; 20:44).

The power of God's hand is mentioned many times in the Bible. However, there are special mentions of the right hand of God. Moses and the Israelites sang of the glorious power of the right hand of God that stretched out and destroyed their enemies (Exodus 15:6-12). God used His mighty hand to make provision for His people. God used Moses' hand with a rod to strike a rock and get water (Numbers 20:11). God's hand is described as having greatness and power (Deuteronomy 3:24; 4:34; Joshua 4:24; I Chronicles 29:12; Psalm 89:13). No one can stand up to the power and greatness of God's hand (II Chronicles 20:6). The hand of God gives strength (Ezra 7:28; Psalm 89:21). The right hand of God does marvelous things (Psalm 98:1). The right hand of God is to be exalted (Psalm 118:16). The Heaven and the earth were created by God's hand (Isaiah 40:12; 48:13).

There are blessings in God's hand. God will pour out blessing on you from Heaven and allow the works of your hand to prosper (Exodus 28:12; 30:9). The hand of

God is good to those who seek Him but against them who forsake Him (Ezra 8:22). Divine favor is referenced as the good hand of God (Nehemiah 2:8; 2:18; Psalm 104:28).

God's hand contains joy, pleasure, marvelous loving kindness, gentleness, saving strength, righteousness, guidance, and help; which will ease your fear. He will hold your hand as you carry out His work (Psalm 16:11; 17:7; 18:35; 20:6; 48:10; 63:8; 73:23; 139:10; Isaiah 41:10; 41:13; 42:6). The shadow of God's hand provides covering for His people (Isaiah 51:16). You are precious in God's hand; like a crown of glory or a royal diadem (Isaiah 62:3).

God uses His hand to transfer His words to you. He will touch your mouth with His hand and put His words in it (Jeremiah 1:9). I can relate this to an experience I had on October 31, 2011 when I was sleeping and felt someone pulling on my mouth. I heard myself called out, "*Jesus!*" in recognition of Who was doing it. I woke up. I stayed awakened for a few minutes and then went back to sleep. I know that the kind of work God charged me to do, will be directed by Jesus Christ Himself. Therefore, He will have to put the words in my mouth as well as direct the use of my hands.

*Chapter 22*

# Spiritual Disruption: Unleashing the Next Wave of Saving Souls

I was in the process of creating the file for this book to send to the printer when The Holy Spirit of God stopped me and led me to a book by James McQuivey from Forrester Research, *Digital Disruption: Unleashing The Next Wave Of Innovation* (McQuivey). I immediately realized that this book was very important to God's work. God wanted me to write about His works in parallel to some of what James had written about his. How I came across this book is a long story. I now share my journey to the discovery of James book with you and the new, spiritually disruptive corporate image of God as He seeks after His children and gather them back to Himself (Ezekiel 34:2-23).

On May 21, 2013, I had a dreamt, which I labeled, *The Line of Defense Vision*. In this dream, *I was on the* street, thinking that I should call my friend to wake him up. I stopped outside a building and started putting something together using a few tools. I heard someone calling my name. I knew that it was coming from the building beside me and that it was from a Japanese man.

A black man came out of the building. I knew that he and others were admiring me. I thought to myself, "It must be that they are seeing God in me." Since the black man came out to me, I decided to go to the Japanese man inside the building. There were many people sitting on benches. I went to where the Japanese man was sitting. As soon as his wife, who was Black, saw me approaching, she left so that I could sit beside him. As I sat beside the Japanese man, I realized I was wearing a highly decorated white dress. I saw that he was also wearing a highly decorated white dress. I told him, "This is how God shows we are angels."

The Japanese man took me outside and showed me a large black hole in the ground. The formation was as if something had landed from the sky and created a huge crater. There were many curious people around. One man decided to go closer and looked in the hole. He was swallowed into the hole.

*After this happened, the Japanese man and I as well as other people started to run away, expecting other things to start happening. We stopped under a building. As we looked back, I saw a building full of restless people who seemed about to rebel.*

*The Japanese man held my right hand and with my left hand, I held on to a woman wearing a highly decorated white dress. The Japanese man held on to someone on his right who was also wearing a highly decorated white dress. A woman in all white dress came up to me and tried to get in the line. I told her she could not join us. I then saw Joan from my church wearing a highly decorated white dress. I told her to join the line. A long line of people with highly decorated white dresses began to form as a defense for the crowd of people behind us. There were many people to my right, who had joined the line. However, I did not get to identify them. We stood in an angelic line as defense of the people, while we waited for things to happen.*

I was reminded of the above dream about a year later when a minister shared her vision during church service on Sunday, June 1, 2014. In her vision, *God woke her up and told her to go and warn the people that He was coming back to New York City. He told her that this time He would open the earth and take everybody – not even the children or babies would be safe.* As she mentioned about the earth opening, I immediately remembered a dream I had about a year ago in which a Japanese man showed me a crater in the earth and we later formed an angelic line of defense for the people.

The minister said she called the bishop of the church to pray for her after telling him the vision. He prayed for her and then told her to go. At first, she didn't know where to go or what to do. As God directed her, she walked the streets near her home and warned those whom she saw. She next took the train and warned people on every car. God told her to remind them of how people jeered and mocked Noah when he was building the ark but ran to him for help when the flood came. God told her to tell the people that they too would be calling for help, but there would be no help.

The minister next said that God told her to go to 42$^{nd}$ Street, Time Square. As I heard her mentioned 42$^{nd}$ Street, The Holy Spirit rose within me. I slapped my hands together very hard and cried out, *"Mighty God, Mighty God."* With this, I realized God had pinpointed the exact area to me. The minister gave the warning to people at 42$^{nd}$ Street, Time Square. As people stared at her, she told them she was a servant of God sent to tell them what God said.

She told them God didn't tell her that He was going to open the earth today or tomorrow and He didn't say Brooklyn, Manhattan, Queens, or the Bronx. But He said He was bringing a disaster back to New York City. She told them to get their hearts right if they were not saved.

After the minister finished her testimony, God put it in my spirit that we should warn the mayor of New York City about it, not just the people. The leaders need to go to God in prayer about this. I know that through prayers, God will handle the earthquake situation, safely for New York City. It is only God Who can prevent Himself from doing what He said He would do. There is always a condition given to us for holding back the *"hand of God."* In this case, it will take political leaders joining with specially connected children of God, in prayer, to prevent the level of disaster God intends for New York City. Although neither the minister nor I prayed with the mayor, we were able to contact him and told him about the vision.

I can relate the minister's experience of going around and warning people of impending disaster to what I did when I took the warning of impending tsunami to my community in Jamaica, West Indies. This was based on the vision of a different minister at my church on Sunday,

March 18, 2012 about a pending tsunami in the area where I grew up.

After hearing the vision about the pending tsunami, I went to Jamaica on vacation. I shared the minister's vision with the people in the community where I grow up. I met a renown dreamer who expressed his belief in the vision and shared his three similar visions. From his visions, I realized that the pending tsunami would be from the devil. After this, I was able to pray against the impending disaster on March 31, 2012, in the sea in Jamaica. I asked God to reverse the tsunami into a Holy Ghost [Spirit] tsunami that starts in my community, extends to the entire country, and then overtakes the entire world.

On Wednesday, April 11, 2012, I returned to America, after missing a previous flight. I read on the internet of the earthquake and tsunami warnings for Indonesia that happened earlier in the day. Not much damage was done by this tsunami, as expected, due to the quake's odd location and size (Stableford). The earthquake was thought to be *"something new...never seen at this level of size in this particular area"* (Than). I knew that because of my prayers in the sea and those from two churches in the area, God diverted the tsunami threat to Indonesia, and handled it safely.

After the minister spoke of her vision about earthquake in New York City, and I connected it to my dream, which I labeled, *The Line of Defense Vision*, God allowed me to hear of an online article about earthquake predictions for Manhattan on July 12$^{th}$ and September 9$^{th}$. This article was related to a book by David Nabhan, *Earthquake – Prediction- Answers In Plain Sight: Times and Dates When the Next Great Tremor Might Strike*. The author is a former science teacher from California who studied earthquakes and claimed that he found the key to accurately predict when one will occur (Daily Mail Reporter).

After seeing the article, about earthquake predictions for Manhattan, I immediately remembered the dream I had in which a Japanese man showed me a large crater in the ground; a man was looking down in it to see what was going to happen and a line of special people formed to defend others from what was expected to happen. David Nabhan represented the man in the dream. I also saw that the article on earthquake predictions was relevant to the minister's testimony about God telling her to warn people that He was coming to New York City; that He would be opening up the earth and no one would escape. Because the article mentioned Manhattan and The Holy

Spirit within me had responded when the minister had mentioned 42$^{nd}$ Street, I immediately felt the urge to share with a high-level manager of the company for which I am working, the vision of the minister at my church and my dream.

The high-level manager at the company for which I work did not disregard what I shared with him. I was not surprised when God used him a few days later to send out information about James McQuivey's book on digital disruption and a link to presentations James had done for the company. The company's high-level manager was encouraging us to come up with innovative ideas, based on what James presented. God used the book summary of this high-level manager to indicate to me that I should acquire James' book and read it.

As I read James book, I saw how God wanted me to realign what I had written for Him with James' work. Within James' book, the strategy God would be using to save souls in masses became clearer to me. Although the regular reader might not see the connection with James' work and that of God's, I can see it. In my experiences with the works of God, it is clear to me that no one is exempt from being used by God. After all, He is the Creator of us and everything else (Genesis 1:1-31; 2:1). God knows that I do not ignore His movements through others. In fact, I embrace it. God even used the title of James' book to guide me to the title of this chapter.

In his book, James pointed out that competitors who are digital disruptors can come from anywhere, disrupting business and stealing consumers; now, imagine a home-based business, which God established to accomplish Holy spiritual disruption, using the concept of digital disruption to save souls. Further, imagine God using someone who knows very little about business to put His spiritually disruptive business in place.

God is full of drama. He is establishing His business in a disruptive way to show that only He, as God, can let it all come together like this. God said that He will use foolish things to confuse the wise and the weak thing of this world to confuse things that seem mighty (1 Corinthians 1:27).

God's strategy of aligning with digital disruption is clear to me. Like the company I am working for, businesses are in the process of changing their mindset to be digitally disruptive to remain viable. It will therefore be easy to transition to a Holy spiritually disruptive mindset, once digital disruption mindset has been established. In a dream, God had told me that His business must be modern. This means that His business will be using digital disruption. However, Holy spiritual disruption will be overriding digital disruption, even though it will ride on digital platforms. I have had many digitally-connected spiritual incidents; some of which are written about in this book and others in my other book, *God's Mission: Spiritual Battles and Revelation of Anti-666*.

I realized that God has used James McQuivey to prepare the business world for accepting digital disruption, which is a segue to Holy spiritual disruption. Like digital disruption, Holy spiritual disruption will be spanning the globe. Companies will have to change some of their products to give consumers the kind of spiritual product experiences they want – experiences that usher in the presence of God. Consumers will be clamoring to deal with companies that are God-conscious. They will want to know the God-status (*Selected, Non-selected*) of companies from which they are buying or dealing with. This means that companies can be "*Selected*" or "*Non-selected*" (*not selected*) by God to do business with.

The God-image of a company as well as the God-like products and services they produce will become important to consumers. The most obvious impact will be on the entertainment industries (music, gaming, movie, etc.) and public media. These industries tend to produce some products that are not Godly in nature. The entertainment industries and public media will have to revamp the fictional stories and characters they present to consumers. Companies must consider if what they are offering consumers give them a spiritually uplifting experience. The question will be, *"Are companies presenting God to consumers who have become spiritually conscious – wanting to indicate whether they are on God's side, or Satan's side?"* A company's Godly image in products and services will be crucial to its survival.

There is Divine favor when companies acknowledge God in doing business. God can take away business from one company and give to another. For example, I have seen a very powerful move of God whereby I realized that He allowed CVS Caremark to get a prescription contract so that when I wanted to find a book about the names of God, I found it at my local CVS pharmacy. The Holy spiritual incident that led me to this happened in less than a year of me having to switch from a pharmacy that sold books, but none about God, to a CVS pharmacy that sold books about God. After I discovered this Godly service at my local CVS pharmacy, I was further impressed when I read about CVS' Godly decision to stop selling tobacco products (Landau).

Once people become aware that they are living in Revelation era, the way they look at businesses will be very different. I know that the seven seals written about in the book of Revelation have been opened. God demonstrated this on November 24, 2013 at my church, as I read Revelation 5 to the congregation. The entire spiritual incident is written about in my book, *God's Mission: Spiritual Battles and Revelation of Anti-666*. The books of Daniel and Revelation, in the Bible, give some ideas of what will be taking place in the spiritually disruptive age – an age in which end-of-time prophecies are fulfilled and people will have to choose if they are accepting, or rejecting the "*mark of the beast.*" Doing business in a Holy spiritually disruptive era will be a challenge. It will require a shift in the mindset of business leaders – one to that of Godly products, services, and experiences.

I know that the business I have established for God will be fully taken over by Jesus Christ of Nazareth, quite soon. As Jesus rides on digital platforms to accomplish His works, those businesses that are not in line with His works will be displaced. Holy Spiritual trend will become consumers' trend as God pour out His Spirit on everyone.

Your children will prophesy; young men will see visions; and old men will have dreams (Acts 2:17). God will be gathering His children and establishing one shepherd (leader) over them because He is not pleased with their situations and how they are being taken care of by current shepherds (Ezekiel 34:2-23). Holy Spiritual disruption will be disrupting digital disruption as God gathers His children.

This gathering of God's children will be taking place from all directions, backgrounds, nationality, and at all ages. You must prepare to be spiritually disrupted. You have no control over this as God opens your spiritual senses to be aware of His works and that of Satan's. Holy Spiritual disruption will be so disruptive that it will shatter some of what we thought were true. We will become not only conscious of the physical world, but also of the spiritual world. After all, God – the head of all principality and power (Colossians 2:10) – will be orchestrating spiritual disruption. The tool of Holy spiritual disruption – The Holy Spirit of God – is available to all who turn away from sin, forgive others who sins against them, ask God for forgiveness of their sins, and accept Jesus Christ as Lord and Savior (2 Corinthians 6:16-18; 2 Peter 3:18; Acts 5:29-32).

## Governments Need Spiritual Disruptors

Even nations will experience Holy spiritual disruption. The country of Jamaica can look forward to being so spiritually disrupted that it will be likened to a *"Holy Ghost [Spirit]"* tsunami. All will see this work of God and glorify Him. Many spiritual incidents led me to say this. I will say a little about them in this book.

Through spiritual incidents, God led me to uncover an article in which Jamaica's Minister of National Security, Peter Bunting, went on his knees and called for Divine intervention as part of the country's crime-fighting strategy (Henry). He had been described by some as being unfit to lead because he is bowing to divinity. The then 51-year-old Jamaica's National Anthem was highlighted as a reason not to seek Divine help. However, I must say this, *"God is faithful, and He is about to honor Peter Bunting's cry for His help into the crime situation in Jamaica."* The Jamaica's National Anthem is about to come alive in a very spiritually disruptive way. Therefore, God wants me to reiterate it in this book.

## Jamaica's National Anthem

*Eternal Father bless our land,*

*Guard us with Thy Mighty Hand, Keep us free from evil powers, Be our light through countless hours.*

*To our Leaders, Great Defender,*

*Grant true wisdom from above.*

*Justice, Truth be ours forever, Jamaica,*

*land we love.*

*Jamaica, Jamaica, Jamaica land we love.*

*Teach us true respect for all,*

*Stir response to duty's call, strengthen us the weak to cherish, Give us vision lest we perish.*

*Knowledge send us Heavenly Father,*

*Grant true wisdom from above.*

*Justice, Truth be ours forever,*

*Jamaica, land we love. Jamaica, Jamaica, Jamaica land we love.*

NOTE: The Anthem is the creative work of four persons, the late Rev. and Hon. Hugh Sherlock, OJ, OBE, the late Hon. Robert Lightbourne, OJ, the late Mapletoft Poulle and Mrs. Poulle (now Mrs. Raymond Lindo).

God did not want me to alter the words of the Jamaica's National Anthem in any way, when writing about it. It was perfectly written and will be perfectly executed for all to recognize that God does answer prayers and that His mighty hand will be guarding Jamaica in a spiritually disruptive way.

I was very pleased to read that Peter Bunting was not deterred from calling on God for help in fighting crime in Jamaica, because of his critics. Instead, he is now conducting lectures about *"Divine intervention into crime"* ("Bunting to deliver lecture on Divine Intervention"). The hallmark of a Holy spiritual disruptor is faith in God and obedience to God. I know that God will honor Peter Bunting's act of faith in publicly requesting His help. Through his leadership, God will reverse the works of Satan in Jamaica and therefore He has brought the cry of Peter Bunting to my attention. Peter Bunting must truly care about the people who he serves to publicly call on God (The Supreme Master of EVERYTHING) for help in correcting the security problems in Jamaica. In a time when governments are adopting anti-God policies, such as removing prayers out of schools, Minister Bunting saw it fit to call on God Who he knows owns EVERYTHING and deserves to be acknowledged in EVERYTHING and should be glorified in EVERYTHING (Psalm 8).

Governments need to re-examine their policies to see if they are edifying God, Who is the owner of the country, or region, which they are governing. Spiritual disruptors need to encourage their governments to call on God in EVERYTHING, but not to include religion in anything. Religion is what causes problem among the children of God. There should be no differentiation, such as Catholic, Presbyterian, Church of God, Seven Day Adventist, etc. when Holy spiritual disruptors are executing the works of God.

The Holy spiritual disruption that is due to take place in Jamaica will spread throughout the world. After I obeyed God and wrote about Peter Bunting and his call for Divine intervention into crimes in Jamaica, God was faithful to allow my sister to tell me about a prayer book she was reading, which mentioned praying to break *"national curses."* I immediately knew I had to pray to break all *"national curses"* that are against Jamaica. I got this information while I was on my way to the beach. As God is *"on time"* with everything, I knew I had to pray in the water for God to break all *"national curses"* that are against Jamaica. I prayed, and this has opened the way for Jamaica's National Anthem to come alive with God guarding Jamaica with His mighty hand.

## A Biblical Example of God's Intervention in Government

The request for Divine intervention into national problems is not new. We have read about many leaders who were not afraid to call on God for help – leaders who rally the people to call on God to save them from danger. There is the example of King Jehoshaphat who was faced with the fearsome armies of the Moab, Ammon, and Meunites. He ordered that a fast (special way of praying to God) be held throughout the country of Judah.

The people obeyed and gathered at the temple in Jerusalem. King Jehoshaphat spoke to God in front of the congregation. He called on God in Heaven, the Ruler of kingdoms on earth; he acknowledged the power and might of God, which no one on earth can withstand. After this, God sent a message to King Jehoshaphat and the people that the battle was His, not theirs. King Jehoshaphat's army won the battle with songs of praises to God which confused the enemy and caused them to destroy each other so that King Jehoshaphat's army did not have to fight face to face with them (2 Chronicles 20:1-24). The battle was won by Holy spiritual disruption with songs of praise to God.

I strongly suggest that world leaders use Holy spiritual disruptions to defeat all the satanic disruptions that have been surfacing around the world, continuously. There are God-selected spiritual disruptors, who world leaders can call on to, along with them, reach out to God for Divine intervention into the situations they are facing. At the time of the draft of this book's manuscript, the U.S. A. president was Obama, and I had said that he would need the help of Holy spiritual disruptors. At the time, he was dealing with a new breed of terrorists and much more. When I was doing battle with the 666 demon, I could relate the experience to a dream I had of President Obama. This is written about in my book, *God's Mission: Spiritual Battles and Revelation of Anti-666*. The experience had led me to believe that maybe President Obama would be in office when manifestation of the *"mark of the beast"* occurs. This did not happen during his presidency, so the presidential figure in the dream is now pointing to the current president.

A lot of questionable disruptions have been happening with the new president, Donald Trump. According to Berglund, a retired firefighter, Mark Taylor, received a prophetic word from God that He chose Donald Trump to lead America (Berglund). This I believe. I can see some things that God is exposing, through this president. I recognize him as an end-time character; most likely representing the rider on the black horse in Revelation 6:5-

6, because of his impact on the economy. I know that Jesus Christ of Nazareth has opened the end-time book in Heaven (Revelation 5:1-9) and is losing the seals (Revelation 6;8). He started demonstrating this while I was reading the scripture from Revelation 5 in church, on Sunday November 24, 2013 (Reid---"God's Mission"). I know that there are more things to be exposed. So, I will continue to watch for manifestation of the *"mark of the beast"* during President Donald Trump reign as president.

Holy spiritual disruption is needed in this government, right now. However, it will be of even greater urgency later. God is faithful to forgive offenses, if people repent and ask Him for forgiveness. We are living in a different era – the end-of-time era; therefore, Holy spiritual disruption should be the tactic used to overcome the works of Satan, through others.

## Spiritual Disruption Platform Is Free

Free, free, free – salvation is free. It comes freely with accepting that Jesus Christ died for your sins, asking forgiveness of your sins, and asking Jesus to enter your heart. Since Jesus came and died for us, everyone must go to God (The Father) through Jesus [The Son] (John 14:6). The evening I started writing about spiritual disruption I went to sleep about 12:30 a.m. I thought I had finished writing about the connection between the works accomplished by James McQuivey on his digital disruption message to the work I was doing on God's Holy spiritual disruption message (McQuivey). However, I had missed a crucial word, *"free."* I have to keep qualifying the *spiritual disruption message* with the word, *"Holy"* because Satan uses people to imitate the works of The Most High God. I know that God will be dealing with those who are falsely representing Him (Revelation 19:20).

God woke me up around 2:30 a.m. to have me write about the *"free"* aspect of His Holy spiritual disruption message. People need to know about *"free"* salvation and about upcoming freedom of worshiping God in spirit and true – without inhibition as to what others may say about them, or think about them. As they receive salvation for free, they will share it with others for free and let it multiply freely. People will freely give testimonies of their spiritual experiences without caring if others think they are crazy. They will have a spiritually disruptive mindset.

People will come to know the truth and the truth will set them free. When Jesus Christ makes us free, we are free indeed (John 8:32; 36). We have sinned, through Adam – the first man; our redemption from sin lies with the gift of Jesus Christ Who died for our sins (Romans 5:14-18). Sinners will receive the gospel that will set them free to become servants of God (Romans 6:18, 6:22-23). The law of the Spirit of Jesus Christ has made us free from the law of sin and death. The righteousness of the law will be fulfilled in us as we seek after the Spirit and not after the physical.

Holy spiritual disruption will become normal and desirable as people seek to become connected to God – their Spiritual Creator (John 4:24). People will learn to differentiate between Godly Spirits and satanic spirits. Satan and his angels are also spirits that were casted out of Heaven and they are amongst us on earth (Revelation 12:9). Holy Spiritual disruption means spiritual freedom. The spiritually wicked works of satanic workers will be exposed; while God's glorious works of healing and deliverance of people from sickness and satanic bondages will uplift the lives of people.

There are many examples in the Bible of the works of Jesus Christ – healing and setting people free from evil and demonic spirits (Matthew 8:16; 9:33). Holy spiritual disruptors, empowered by God, will be even more disruptive as they continue the works of Jesus to heal and deliver people (John 14:12). To be a very effective Holy spiritual disruptor you must exercise faith in God and be obedient to Him. Lack of faith and disobedience are barriers to achieving Holy spiritual disruption. Those who are true Holy spiritual disruptors will have their stories of being tried and proven by God and of going through fire and water (Psalm 66:10-12). At times Holy spiritual disruptors will need to be obedient in forming temporary alliances to accomplish a task for God.

Holy spiritual disruptors will be turning our world upside down, including social and commercial aspects of it. There will be major impacts on the healthcare industry as healing and deliverance take place in the lives of people. There will be major impacts on the entertainment industries as spiritual consumers shape the market by requiring Godly entertainment, products, and services. The younger generation is also a part of God's call to be spiritually disruptive. Jesus called me when I was about four years old. It was only a few years ago that I realized this calling on my life was to be an *"end-of-time"* leader of Holy spiritual disruption. Based on my experiences with God, a major part of His work is done through the spirit.

When we are in the physical, we cannot please God. You need the Spirit of God and the Spirit of Jesus Christ to live in you so that you can be identified as His own.

Children of God are led by His Spirit and His Spirit will witness to our spirit to identify us as His children (Romans 8:2-16).

The Spirit of God heals us. At times, we are not sure what to pray for, but His Spirit within us communicate with Him with groaning about things that cannot be spoken. God knows our hearts and knows what His Spirit within us wants to speak to Him about (Romans 8:26). We need to be prepared for a time of spiritual freedom; a time when we accept the gift of everlasting life from Jesus Christ and let the Spirit of God live in us and intercede on our behalves, to Him. People will feel free to share the gospel of Jesus Christ. They will become righteous (right with God) instead of religious because religion causes separation in the Body of Christ.

Let the Spirit of God flows freely from one to the other as He executes His works through us. God's work is not about an individual, but about the *"Body of Christ."* Each of us is just a member of the *"Body of Christ"* (1 Corinthians 12:27-31) and must work together so that our parts can contribute to the whole plan of God. Salvation is given for free by Jesus Christ; let us pass it on for free to others as we openly share our spiritual experiences of God.

## A Spiritually Disruptive Business

Holy spiritual disruption comes with the awakening of spiritual senses. After awakening my spiritual senses, God trained me to recognize when He is working in a situation. That is why I can recognize when He is using someone to accomplish His works, even if the individual is not aware of it. Be ready for your own spiritual awakening. Holy spiritual disruption is not new. However, it is the speed at which it will be happening that will be new.

Holy spiritual disruption will spread like wildfire when God brings His business, Works Of Trinity, LLC, to the public. I know that the work I am establishing for God has to do with the return of Jesus Christ. The stories I have about this warrants the writing of another book. As one of my very highly Godly anointed niece prayed for me, God used her to confirm that the works I am doing is related to the return of Jesus Christ. After all, He must come back to deal with *"666 demon,"* commonly known as the *"mark of the beast"* (Revelation 19; 13:18).

I am aware that Jesus has given me a tremendous amount of work to do on His behalf, some I have already accomplished, some I am currently working on, and others I don't even know about, yet. The magnitude of the work ahead of me was revealed in a dream on October 28, 2010, in which *my cousin, Lea, showed me a list of things Jesus wanted her to have. I then found myself with a long list of things, which I knew Jesus wanted me to have. In the dream, I was thinking that I didn't know about them.*

In another dream on November 8, 2010, it was revealed to me that in the end, Jesus would literally completely take over the work I had started for Him. In this dream, *I was in a large room with a woman standing by a blackboard at the other end. This woman asked, "Who will die for Jesus?" I, as well as another woman in the room said we would. I didn't see the woman; I only become aware of her and heard her response. I waited for a while, feeling ready to die for Jesus. The woman at the blackboard threw lighter fluid on me. I expected to be consumed by fire and die. However, I did not see any fire and was surprised I didn't die.*

*As I wondered why I was still alive, I saw Jesus. He was medium built, handsome, and as black as charcoal – like a typical African. I knew he was in the fire with me although I didn't see any fire. I realized Jesus was very black because of the fire.*

*I next became aware that God was in the room. He appeared as a man, to the left of me. However, I could not see His face. God handed me a black business bag which I* could tell was an older type. God said, "It should be the modern one." I took the bag and passed it to Jesus.

As indicated by this dream, I will pass on the task of directing God's company to Jesus Christ. I am just putting things in place for Him to take over the running of Works Of Trinity, LLC. God demonstrated this in the following spiritual incident.

Since I was not too knowledgeable about business, I searched for information on the internet on, *"starting a business."* I realized that for a LLC, I would have to create an *"Operating Agreement."* As such, I bought a template geared towards the State in which I wanted to incorporate. The template allows you to insert your customized information at certain points in the document. While customizing the template, I came across the *"Article 1 – Organization"* section with the *"Purpose"* sub-section. In this sub-section, you are required to insert, *"business activity/activities"* the company will be engaged in. I decided not to directly type in the document, but first sort out my thoughts in a temporary document and then cut and paste the final version into the Operating Agreement document. Here I see not only me, but God also creating this Operating Agreement.

After I finalized what I wanted to put as the business activities, I copied it from the temporary document. In the Operating Agreement document, I placed the cursor where I wanted to paste the text. However, when I clicked the paste button, there was an unusual movement of the words. I carefully looked to see what happened. I noticed that the information I pasted was placed in two parts of the paragraph instead of one. It was intentionally inserted, by spiritual incident, after the words, *"engaged in and organized under the Act as approved by."* I complied with God's direction and have the purpose read as follows:

*"The purposes of the Company shall be to engage in promotion of the works of God, Jesus, and the Holy Spirit through publishing/sale of books and company branded merchandise online, at special organized events, and any other lawful business or activity for which the limited liability company may be engaged in and organized under the Act as approved by God, Jesus, and the Holy Spirit and by the Board of Managers or the Members."*

This spiritual incident of God defining the purpose of Works Of Trinity, LLC is yet again reassurance that God is with me in executing His business, every step of the way. He will be controlling both the spiritual and physical aspects of His business.

Works Of Trinity, LLC will be radically different in the way the gospel is spread globally – I now call it Holy spiritual disruption. It will be combining the power of the Trinity (God, Jesus, The Holy Spirit) and the power of commerce to bring healing to individuals in unique ways. The identity of Works Of Trinity, LLC will be known throughout the world. It is one that God Himself has put together for me to establish for Him; one that will create a Holy spiritual disruption, which the world has never seen before. God even made astounding spiritual connection when I visited Israel in November 2016.

Before leaving for Israel, on Sunday, October 2016, I was in church when the bishop started encouraging us to forget about the past. He asked us to participate in an exercise to erase the past. He told us to get a pen and start to write in the air. After this he told us to turn the pen around and start to erase. We all participated as instructed. At home before I fell asleep, I suddenly started performing the act of writing in the air, using my right hand. I knew I was doing this because of what had happened in church earlier. I thought about the books I was writing. I started speaking in tongues while writing in the air. The Holy Spirit then spoke out, through me. I could tell that He was angry. In a very strong voice I spoke out, *"Heavenly*

*Father, recall your words and let them devour the words of the enemy.*" I would remember this incident when I visited Israel

In November 2016, by God's doing, I visited Israel. I felt that Jesus Christ wanted me to see where He was born and spent His physical life on earth. I made a few outstanding Holy spiritually disruptive connections with my visit to Israel and what I am doing for God. While at the top of Masada, as we walked around the tour guide would explain the history of each area. We were at an area which he said was the site of a synagogue. He said they knew that because fragments of two scrolls were found. When he said that Ezekiel 35 was found and the writing about "*dry bones*" was intact, my spirit reacted. I raised my right hand in the air and started to praise God, quietly. I immediately remembered the spiritual incident, I mentioned above, with Holy Spirit strongly recalling the words of God and speaking that they should devour the words of the enemy. I must pause here to review Ezekiel 35 because it has end-time implications.

The Lord took Ezekiel to a valley which was filled with dry bones and asked him if the bones can live. After Ezekiel told the Lord that He knew. The Lord took told Ezekiel to prophesy to the dry bones and to tell them to hear the word of the Lord; that the Lord said He would put sinews and flesh on them, cover them with skin, breath in them and they would live. Ezekiel prophesied as the Lord commanded. First, sinews and flesh came on them and they were covered with skin, but there was no breath.

The Lord told Ezekiel to prophesy to the wind and tell it that the Lord said it should come from the four winds, as breath, and breathe on the slain so that they might live. Ezekiel prophesied to the wind and breath came on the slain and they lived and stood up on their feet, as an exceedingly great army. The Lord told Ezekiel that the dry bones represented His children of Israel. The Lord told Ezekiel to tell them He would open their graves, cause them to come out of them, and bring them into Israel; because of this, they will know that He is their God. He will put His Spirit in them and they would live; God would place them in their own land and they would know the God spoke it and did it (Ezekiel 37:1-14).

In another Divine spiritual incident, while touring Israel, I learned that fish was the first symbol of Christianity which was later switched to the cross; and that the oldest Christian churches were established in the year 333. Hearing about the switching of symbols for Christianity and 333 as the year for establishing Christian churches reminded me of when God indicated that I should switch the draft of His business logo, which has 333 incorporated, from a cross to a star. The detail of the story is in chapter 7.

In Bethlehem, while touring the Church of the Nativity, I was surprised to see two very old wooden carvings of Jesus Christ, as a Black man. This reminded me of the charcoal color of Jesus Christ in the dream I mentioned earlier in this chapter, in which I was passing the business bag God gave me to Him. This spiritually disruptive connection to my dream caused me to wonder if all will gladly receive Jesus Christ when He returns in the color He had while in His physical body on earth.

After I returned from Israel, God confirmed a prophecy I got earlier that I was a pastor. After the confirmation, He gave me a dream in which He used the bishop of my church to give me stones; like the pendants I bought with symbols of the fish and cross, to indicate that I should establish His end-time church. I immediately knew that this would be a church without borders and that it was symbolic of the corporate business I established for God. In His business, God will have the liberty to take care of His sheep (children) as He pleases. I also realized that the symbol for the end-time church is the logo which God had me design for His business.

The many spiritual incidents that formed many little stories, as retold in this book, give others an insight into how God conducts His business. By dreams and spiritual incidents God directs and move things in the direction He wants them to go. God controls everything and everybody from every angle, and nothing escapes Him. Spiritual incidents are what others might call coincidence. However, when I see the hallmark of God putting things together, I call them spiritual incidents. Holy spiritual disruptions will involve spiritual incidents, as God orchestrate His works through His chosen spiritual disruptors.

# Bibliography

American Psychological Association. "Violent music lyrics increase aggressive thoughts and feelings, according to new study; even humorous violent songs increase hostile feelings." *ScienceDaily*, 5 May 2003. Web. 12 Dec. 2011.

Berglund, Taylor. "Prophecy from 2011 Claims Trump Was Chosen By God to Save America." *Charisma News. 14 June 2016.* Accessed 14 October 2016. http://www.charismanews.com/opinion/57774-prophecy-from-2011-claims-trump-was-chosen-by-god-to-save-america.

Brown, Rebecca., MD. *He Came To Set The Captives Free.* Whitaker House, 1986.

"Bunting to deliver lecture on 'Divine Intervention'." *News. Jamaica Observer, Tuesday, April 15, 2014.* Web. Accessed 9 May 2014. http://www.jamaicaobserver.com/pfversion/Bunting-to-deliver-lectureon--Divine-Intervention-

Capps, Charles. *God Creative Power: Will Work for You.* Harrison House, 1976.

Daily Mail Reporter. 1 June 2014. "The man who says he's worked out how to PREDICT earthquakes and says the next one to hit U.S. will be on July 12". *Mail Online.* Accessed 11 April 2012. http://www.dailymail.co.uk/news/article-2645369/Author-claims-able-predict-earthquakes-says-one-U-S-July-12.html.

Dreisinger, Baz. "Insight vs. incite." *Los Angeles Times. 17 July 2005.* Web. Accessed 12 Dec. 2011.

# Bibliography

Eldred, Ken. *God is at Work.* Manna Ventures, LLC, 2009.

Henry, M. "Divine intervention for crime reduction." *The Gleaner. Jamaica, West Indies. 11 August 2011.* Web. Accessed 31 December 2013. http://jamaica-gleaner.com/gleaner/20130811/focus/ focus4.html.

Isaacs, Kimiela. *Joshua.* Produced by Diana Morrison. 2010. CD.

Landau, Elizabeth. "CVS stores to stop selling tobacco." *CNN Health. CNN, Wed February 5, 2014.* Web. Accessed 2 September 2014. http://www.cnn.com/2014/02/05/ health/cvs-cigarettes

Lewis, Lester, and Singing Rose Ministry. *Golden Sceptre.* Ministries International. n.d. CD.

Martino, Steven, et al. *Exposure to Degrading Versus Nondegrading Music Lyrics and Sexual. Behavior Among Youth.* RAND.org. 01 January 2006. Web. Accessed 01 January 2018. https://www.rand.org/pubs/external_publications/EP20060803.html.

McQuivey, James. *Digital Disruption: Unleashing the Next Wave of Innovation.* Amazon Publishing, 2013.

# Bibliography

Morningstar, Robert. 'The UFO Digest Spotlight on: The national press club conference on "UFO's & Nukes."' 27 September 2010. Web. Accessed 6 October 2010. http://www.ufodigest.com/article/ufo-digest-spotlight-national-press-club-conference-ufos-nukes.

Palmer, A. "Violent song lyrics may lead to violent behavior." *American Psychological Association*, vol. 34, no. 7, 2003, p. 15. Web. Accessed 12 December 2011.

Phillips, Chuck. 'Rap defense doesn't stop death penalty: 'The music affected me,' says Ronald Ray Howard. "That's how it was that night I shot the trooper."' *Los Angeles Times*. 15 July 1993. Web. Accessed 12 Dec. 2011.

Prosnitz, H. "1775 Windsor Road: Arts Center Proposed for Vacant Site." *Teaneck Surbanite*. 2010.

"Rare star-making galaxy found." Web. Accessed 29 September 2010. www.Astronomy.com.

Reid, Jenness. *God Works Through Dreams.* Works Of Trinity, LLC, 2018. [---].

---. *God's Mission: Spiritual Battles and Revelation of Anti-666.* Works Of Trinity, LLC, 2018.

Roth, Sid. Interview with Joyner, Rich. *Guest: Rich Joyner.* TV. Accessed 7 January 2011. https://sidroth.org/television/tv-archives/rick-joyner/

# Bibliography

Stableford, Dylan. "Indonesia earthquake: Ttsunami warnings issued after 8.6 magnitude quake strikes off coast." *The Envoy*. Accessed 11 April 2012. http://news.yahoo.com/blogs/envoy/indonesia-earthquake-ttsunami-warnings-issued-massive-quakes-strike-131634257.html.

Sorger, Matt. "Awakening: The invasion of God into our culture." *Matt Sorger Ministries*. April 2006. Web. Accessed 13 January 2012 http://www.mattsorger.com/teachings.aspx?id=27. [---].

---. *Sustaining A Permanent Change*. MSM Monthly CD Teaching. Matt Sorger Ministries. n.d. CD.

---. *The Finished Work*. MSM Monthly CD Teaching. Matt Sorger Ministries. n.d. CD.

Than, Ker. "No Tsunami? Why Earthquake Spared Indonesia Today [4/11/2012]: Quake's odd location and size makes it 'something new,' expert says," *National Geographic Daily News*. Accessed 11 April 2012. http://news.nationalgeographic.com/news/2012/04/12 0411-tsunami-alert-watch-warning-earthquake-indonesia-aceh-science-/.

*The Holy Bible*. King James Version. Holman Bible Publishers, 1979.

# Bibliography

Todd, John. "The illuminati and witchcraft: Part II." n.d. Web. Accessed 18 February 2012. http://kt70.com/~jamesjpn/articles/john_todd_and_the_illuminati_2.htm.

"US politician dabbled in witchcraft, tape reveals." *Deccan Chronicle On The Web*. 2010. Web. Accessed 13 January 2011.

"Worship." *Merriam-Webster*. Web. Accessed 12 January 2012. http://www.merriam-webster.com/dictionary/worship.

Yoder, Barbara. *Gathering of the Eagles Summit*. vol. II, Session #5, 2011. MSM Matt Sorger Ministries. DVD.

Zambrano, Angelica. "Prepare to meet your God!" 2011. Web. Accessed 23 February 2012. http://spiritlessons.com/Documents/Prepare_to_meet_your_God/index.htm.

www.ingramcontent.com/pod-product-compliance
Lightning Source LLC
Chambersburg PA
CBHW020646300426
44112CB00007B/258